AMERICAN HOR~~TICULTURAL SOCIETY~~   SL
PRACT~~ICAL GUIDES~~ 2 9-01

BULBS

AMERICAN HORTICULTURAL SOCIETY
PRACTICAL GUIDES

BULBS

Rod Leeds

A Dorling Kindersley Book

Dorling DK Kindersley

LONDON, NEW YORK, SYDNEY, DELHI, PARIS, MUNICH and JOHANNESBURG

SERIES EDITOR Annelise Evans
SERIES ART EDITOR Ursula Dawson
US EDITOR Ray Rogers
MANAGING EDITOR Anna Kruger
MANAGING ART EDITOR Lee Griffiths
DTP DESIGNERS Louise Paddick, Louise Waller
PRODUCTION MANAGER Sarah Coltman

Produced for Dorling Kindersley by

studio cactus

13 SOUTHGATE STREET WINCHESTER HAMPSHIRE SO23 9DZ
SENIOR EDITOR Jane Baldock
SENIOR DESIGNER Sharon Moore

First American Edition, 2001
2 4 6 8 10 9 7 5 3 1
Published in the United States by
Dorling Kindersley Publishing, Inc., 95 Madison Avenue, New York, NY 10016

Dorling Kindersley Publishing, Inc. offers special discounts for bulk purchases for sales
promotions or premiums. Specific, large-quantity needs can be met with special editions,
including personalized covers, excerpts of existing guides, and corporate imprints.
For more information, contact Special Markets Department, Dorling Kindersley
Publishing, Inc., 95 Madison Avenue, New York, NY 10016 Fax: 800-600-9098

Library of Congress Cataloging-in-Publication Data

Leeds, Rod
Bulbs / Rod Leeds
    p. cm. -- (AHS practical guides)
    Includes index.
    ISBN 0-7894-7126-4 (alk. paper)
    1. Bulbs.
    I. American Horticultural Society II. Title. III. Series

SB425 .L366 2001
635.9'4--dc21   00-056041

Reproduced by Colourscan, Singapore
Printed and bound by Star Standard Industries PTE Ltd, Singapore

see our complete catalog at

www.dk.com

CONTENTS

BULBS IN THE GARDEN 7

An introduction to using bulbs for year-round color. How to choose bulbs for cut flowers or dried seedheads. Using bulbs to provide fragrance, color, and structure in the garden.

PLANTING PLANS FOR BULBS 32

LOOKING AFTER YOUR BULBS 48

Buying healthy bulbs, preparing the soil and planting, routine care and maintenance, how to store bulbs, forcing prepared bulbs, growing your own bulbs, and avoiding problems.

CHOICE BULBS FOR THE GARDEN 64

A photographic guide to a selection of some of the best garden bulbs, including information on hardiness, moisture requirements, and flowering times.

USING BULBS IN THE GARDEN

WHAT ARE BULBS?

BULB IS A GENERAL TERM used by gardeners for plants with a food-storage organ that allows them to grow and flower quickly once the optimum conditions occur. They may be true bulbs, such as daffodils and lilies; corms, such as crocuses; tubers, such as cyclamens and dahlias; or rhizomes, such as wood anemones. These "bulbs" all exist for different reasons and have different flowering and resting periods.

SEASONAL CHOICES

For the gardener, there is a huge and colorful array of bulbs for every season of the year. Many of these are quite hardy, but some, such as cannas, are more tender and are grown in the same way as seasonal bedding plants. In cold climates, frost-tender plants need to be cultivated in a frost-free greenhouse or conservatory.

Fortunately, many bulbous plants can be grown easily in temperate climates, such as in North America, if the gardener plans position and site to his or her advantage.

Each bulb is a highly condensed plant, whose embryonic roots, stem, leaves, and flower(s) are all contained within it, just waiting for the appropriate moisture and temperature conditions for growth to begin.

AUTUMN COLOR Cyclamen hederifolium *is an attractive autumn-flowering cyclamen that looks very good when planted in groups or drifts.*

◄ RUBY TULIPS *Planted in solid blocks of color, tulips and grape hyacinths make a strong impact.*

BULBS FOR ALL SEASONS

VERY VERSATILE AND EASILY GROWN PLANTS, bulbs can provide color from some of the most graceful of garden flowers throughout the year. Traditionally we think of the highlights produced by bulbs such as daffodils in spring and the stately tulips that follow, but there are many more bulbs to consider. The vast range of bulbs available provides flowers from across the color spectrum for every month of the year.

SPRING

This is the one season when even non-gardeners view with appreciation the bulb's efforts to drive away the winter blues.

It is possible to have daffodils flowering in the garden for over two months. The season starts with selections such as *Narcissus* 'February Gold' in early spring. The beautiful white 'Thalia' follows in mid-spring and the sweetly scented double white 'Cheerfulness' a little later. One of the last daffodils to flower is 'Tripartite', which has several golden yellow flowers per stem and often looks its best in late spring.

Tulips provide some of the most vibrant flower shades, with hues ranging from yellow through orange to red and violet. White tulips can be used to tone down and give welcome contrast to the brighter flowers. The medium and shorter varieties are less inclined to bend in inclement weather, and tulips such as *T.* 'Purissima' and *T.* 'White Triumphator' stand proudly over smaller spring flowers.

The choice of other bulbs in spring is enormous. There are the small Reticulata irises, in mostly blues and purples, and the pure blue of the scillas and glory of the snow (*Chionodoxa*), which soon carpet the ground through their seed production. Widening the range can be achieved by growing the little South American *Ipheion uniflorum* 'Wisley Blue', a pale blue, starry flower that rises above its leaves. Other shades are becoming available for this plant. A similar effect can be achieved by growing *Anemone blanda*, often blue, but also available in white, purple, and red.

SPRING BULBS

Chionodoxa forbesii
Ipheion uniflorum cultivars
Narcissus 'Dove Wings'
Narcissus 'Irene Copeland'
Narcissus 'Jack Snipe'
Narcissus 'Jetfire'
Narcissus 'Minnow'
Narcissus 'Mount Hood'
Scilla siberica 'Spring Beauty'
Tulipa linifolia Batalinii Group
Tulipa praestans 'Fusilier'

NODDING DAFFODILS
The small-flowered Narcissus *'Jack Snipe' and* Anemone blanda *have a grace and beauty that is never overbearing.*

RIOT OF RED
The bright flowers of Anemone pavonina *are showstoppers in spring. They thrive in the sunniest and driest spot in the garden.*

SUMMER

With the arrival of summer there are, ideally, no bare patches of soil: either the gardener has planted a tapestry of species, or nature has done the same. For bulbs to make an impact at this time of year they must be tall and well able to fend for themselves in the jungle of foliage. This

ARTFUL ALLIUMS
The pompon-headed alliums are excellent garden plants. Purple here, but also available in white, blue, and yellow, these bulbs fill in nicely between herbaceous plants in late spring.

SUMMER BULBS

Allium giganteum
Allium 'Globemaster'
Camassia cusickii
  'Zwanenburg'
Camassia leichtlinii
  'Semiplena'
Galtonia candicans
Lilium 'Karen North'
Lilium 'Marie North'
Lilium martagon var. album

dense summer cover can, however, often be useful, since some taller bulb foliage becomes rather ragged by summer and is best hidden by surrounding plants. Alliums, camassias, and galtonias fall into this category, but their globes and spires add interest to any border, although they work particularly well when grown in conjunction with herbaceous plants.

The tender bulbs can now be planted out or left in their pots to decorate patios or pathways. Bulbs such as cannas, gladioli, and dahlias are very colorful and can create dramatic effects. Lilies begin to rise in the borders at this time of year, showing off their attractive stems and leaves. The hybrid lilies are often the easiest to grow, but they may lack some of the beauty of the species. Often referred to as the giant lily, *Cardiocrinum giganteum* loves a rich, moist situation, when its stems – bearing heart-shaped leaves and scented trumpet flowers – may reach heights of up to 6ft (2m) to form a spectacular sight.

AUTUMN

Many autumn bulbs produce flowers on naked stems, their leaves developing in the following spring. When they are planted (in late summer, earlier than spring bulbs), the space that will be taken by their leaves the following year needs to be considered, for some – like the colchicums and amaryllis – have abundant and far-reaching foliage. Nerines and amaryllis lead the way. Both flower profusely if planted under a sunny wall, with the bulb tops just visible. They have pink, and occasionally white, trumpet-shaped flowers held on thick stems.

The ivy-leaved cyclamen, *Cyclamen hederifolium*, is superb when grown in drifts; its mixed white and pink flowers are soon followed by beautiful green- and silver-patterned leaves. Providing a complete contrast in color are the sternbergias, with bright yellow goblet-shaped flowers. Lovers of hot, sunny spots, they bloom over a long period, with some lingering into winter.

Often referred to as "autumn crocuses" are the colchicums, which are in the same family as daffodils (*Narcissus*) and usually pink, a color never achieved by a true crocus. Colchicums look very effective when grown in groups in quite wide borders, planted to allow enough space for the leaves to develop in spring.

Closely planted autumn bulbs brighten up a tired garden after the summer

Colchicum speciosum 'Album' is a crystalline white goblet above a lime green stem – a perfect combination with a good constitution able to resist the vagaries of autumn weather. Last to be admired here is a real autumn crocus, *Crocus speciosus* 'Oxonian', a rich dark purple flower that is very tolerant of planting position.

ALTERNATIVE FOR AUTUMN
The South African Eucomis *are reliable late summer and autumn flowerers. They make ideal container plants.*

AUTUMN BULBS

Amaryllis belladonna
Colchicum byzantinum
Colchicum speciosum
 'Album'
Colchicum 'Waterlily'
Crocus speciosus 'Oxonian'
Dahlia (all cultivars)
Lilium speciosum
Nerine bowdenii
Sternbergia lutea

▲ SPLASH OF PINK
Colchicums are easy to grow and effective flowers for prolonging interest in autumn borders, either as an edging or filling between plants.

▶ A WINTER BORDER
Cyclamen coum, with all its colors and leaf markings, makes a very interesting bed in winter. It is easy in every respect and deserves to be more widely grown.

WINTER

At this time of year, the cultivation of bulbs for indoor decoration is very popular. Traditionally, prepared hyacinths and daffodils (*Narcissus*) have long been the stalwarts for brightening up the season, but gaining a larger share of the market are the amaryllis (*Hippeastrum*), large-flowered hybrids that can be planted in autumn to flower in the depths of winter.

In milder climates it is possible to have bulbs in flower right through the winter, cheering all who pass their carpets of color. It is best to plan these winter plantings along the sides of pathways for ease of access. If the bed can be raised, so much the better, for the scents can then be appreciated. The snowdrop (*Galanthus*) is an amazing little bulb, tough, easily grown,

and with different varieties that can be in flower from mid-autumn through to early spring. The common snowdrop (*Galanthus nivalis*) is a great survivor and is found naturalized in older gardens. Try to find a supplier who sells these bulbs "in the green," which means they are still in leaf and offered as flowering finishes. The survival rate of these bulbs is usually far greater than if you plant dry bulbs bought in summer.

Equally impressive in winter are the winter aconites (*Eranthis*), little yellow flowers surrounded by ruffs of leaves that break through the soil at the first sign of warmth. The winter-flowering cyclamen, *Cyclamen coum*, is marvelous as an impact plant, and its magenta to white flowers are surprisingly resistant to cold.

BULBS FOR PICKING

PICKED FLOWERS SHOW OFF the marvelous intricacies of their markings and scent so that they can be fully appreciated. Even if you are not a flower arranger, a simple slim vase is perfectly adequate, even for a single bloom. Some flowers do not open fully outside if the temperature or light intensity are low. This is particularly relevant during the winter months, when both of these problems can be overcome easily in the warmth of a house.

CUT-FLOWER SELECTION
The amazing arrangements seen at flower shows give an idea of the types of bulb that can be grown for picking. If you pick regularly, it is best to grow the bulbs exclusively for this purpose as part of the vegetable garden. Bulbs, such as gladioli, are excellent as cut flowers but are hard to place in an informal garden, so if you plant them in rows between the onions and carrots you can grow them with your vegetables.

CUTTING AND KEEPING FLOWERS
When selecting stems for cutting, pick those in loose bud and take only the length you need, leaving as many leaves as possible so that the bulb can be built up for the following year. Be sure to cut the stem at an acute angle so that it can draw up as much water as possible and thereby remain fresh longer. Put the flowers in a cool place in warm water, and remove any leaves that might be completely underwater to prevent them from rotting. Use one of the brands of commercial flower preservatives that prolong the life of the stem, or add a teaspoon of sugar and a dash of bleach.

The water in cut-flower arrangements should be replaced every other day to help keep it fresh-smelling, and dying flowerheads need to be removed to keep the arrangement looking attractive for

---

Smaller bulbs can be used to make exquisite individual arrangements

---

longer. Many bulbs – including amaryllis, nerines, and lilies – are excellent in flower arrangements, being both long-lasting and having rigid stems. Note that lily pollen can stain clothing, so be aware of this both when placing lilies in the garden and when arranging cut lilies. It is preferable to retain the stamens, if possible, since they provide a nice contrasting feature.

ELEGANT ANEMONES
Anemones make long-lasting cut flowers. Here they are tied tightly, making an unusual and eye-catching arrangement.

SINGLE STEMS
Tulips are excellent as cut flowers and hold themselves well. Cut the stems as long as possible with their leaves and with the flowers in bud, and they will always open.

Make sure you cut the stem below the point at which the leaves are attached

SEASONAL ARRANGEMENTS

An old custom of combining flowers and foliage for a particular event was revived early on in the 20th century by the great gardeners Vita Sackville-West and Lady Scott. This simple arrangement, called a tussie-mussie, has its origins as a form of nosegay that was used to disguise unpleasant odors. Today, luckily, this purpose is rarely necessary, but the gathering of flowers for an occasion is

always a pleasure. During the quieter times of the year, and particularly in winter, it is often a challenge for the gardener to gather flowers. The search can be surprisingly rewarding, however, especially if the snow is not too deep, since maybe to be found are sternbergias, crocuses, snowdrops (*Galanthus*), and cyclamens, while forced daffodil (*Narcissus*) and hyacinth blooms can also be included.

Flowers gathered for a winter arrangement can be surrounded by evergreens in a simple arrangement set in a shallow bowl.

DAFFODIL "TREE"
A stunning use of daffodils. These flowers have short coronas (centers) and make ideal subjects for a tight ball arrangement.

BULBS FOR FLORISTRY

Allium cristophii
Allium hollandicum
Crocosmia × *crocosmiiflora* 'Dusky Maiden'
Crocosmia × *crocosmiiflora* 'Star of the East'
Dahlia (all cultivars)
Gladiolus Grandiflorus Group
Leucojum aestivum 'Gravetye Giant'
Lilium (all)
Narcissus (all)
Nerine bowdenii
Tulipa (all)

BULBS WITH DECORATIVE SEEDHEADS

T HE MORE BULBS YOU GROW, the more you will find that they leave an attractive legacy at the end of the summer, namely the dry seedhead that may also be full of seed. The most familiar seedhead is that of the allium, which is spherical and designed to break off the stem and be blown around arid plains, shedding seeds as it goes. Most of the seedheads that naturally become rigid with age do so as an adaptation for seed dispersal, usually by wind.

DRYING BULB SEEDHEADS

The moist conditions in autumn begin the process of decay, leaving the gardener the choice of picking and drying, or leaving the seedheads in situ. The time for harvesting seedheads depends upon the dryness of the head, which is always best pulled after a dry, sunny day. Once harvested, the stems need to be hung in a dry, airy place for a few weeks so that they can continue to dry and shed their seeds. One method is to place the seedheads in large paper (not plastic) bags, so that, as

> ## The seedheads of alliums are ideal for drying

GARDEN GLOBES
The old flowerheads of alliums make effective dried spherical globes for an everlasting display.

When dried, the seeds may become trapped in the capsules of the flowerhead

the seeds are released from the chambers, they will be caught in the bag and will be ready to sow. When you remove the seeds, look out for insects that may have emerged from the seed capsules as they dried.

SUITABLE BULBS

Many alliums – including *Allium atropurpureum, A. hollandicum, A. rosenbachianum,* and *A. schubertii* – are ideal for preserving as dried flowerheads, and each differs in height and structure, something you notice only at close quarters. If the heads are not gathered, they look very beautiful covered in frost and may remain well into winter before they finally snap and collapse. An unusual way to display seedheads like those of *Allium hollandicum* 'Purple Sensation' is to plant long drifts of them through the border. Attractive in summer, they have pompon seedheads in autumn.

The taller fritillaries, tulips, and some lilies form larger capsules that contain flat, lighter seed that drifts away in the breeze once the seed case opens. These capsules can also be harvested as soon as the leaves turn brown and can be dried in the same way as alliums. You may, however, need to strip off any remaining leaves attached to the stems before they are displayed.

The most imposing of all bulbous seedheads is seen on the stem of the giant lily, *Cardiocrinum giganteum*, from Asia. Its large, hollow stem is thick and very tall, and after the seeds are gathered, it can be placed in a container to dry. Cardiocrinum seed capsules are large and have three sides, each edged with teeth that look rather like the teeth on a Venus flytrap. The teeth hold to the seeds until the wind is strong enough for there to be a reasonable chance of distant seed dispersal. Dried cardiocrinum seedheads are so strong and durable that the hardest task in preserving them is deciding how best to keep them free of dust.

SEEDHEAD CHOICES

Allium cristophii
Allium hollandicum
Allium hollandicum
  'Purple Sensation'
Allium
  'Globemaster'
Allium nigrum
Allium schubertii
Fritillaria (all)
Tulips (all)

FRITILLARIA SEEDHEADS

Dried seedheads are very long lasting and can be used in mixed dried-flower arrangements, or within fresh arrangements provided that the stems do not reach the water (otherwise, they will begin to rot). Alternatively, dried seedheads can also be colored with spray paint for festive decorations or for children's creations.

GONE TO SEED
Some seedheads, such as this cardiocrinum, can be left to dry in the open garden until such time as they are needed for use in dried decorations. These dried capsules and the hollow stem are very substantial and can be up to 6ft (2m) tall when eased from the ground.

BULBS FOR FOLIAGE

THE LEAVES OF BULBS are often regarded as their greatest drawback, taking weeks to die down and looking unsightly as they yellow with age. Daffodils are the most reviled in this respect, so much so that trials have been conducted to see how soon their leaves can be removed without affecting subsequent flowering. Other bulbs, however, produce leaves that can provide additional interest, giving dramatic structure and color to borders.

LEAVING THE LEAVES

Bulb leaves fall into three categories: those, such as daffodils, that need hiding or just ignoring; those, such as crocuses and corydalis, which are so fleeting once the sun becomes stronger in spring that they soon wither and virtually disappear; and, luckily, a third group with attractive foliage that is pleasing in its own right. Of the latter, some have leaves that complement the flowers, while others – usually autumn-flowering bulbs – make their leaf growth the following spring. Whenever the leaves develop, do not be tempted to remove them until they begin to turn yellow, when their job is finished. In the case of daffodils, it is recommended that you leave the leaves for six weeks, and do not tie or knot them.

> Architectural leaves can make a stunning impact before flowering occurs

The combination of leaves and flowers in some bulbs is worth considering. Dog's-tooth violets (*Erythronium*) have broad, often mottled leaves that emerge prior to flowering. All cyclamens have attractive leaves, particularly the autumn-flowering species *C. hederifolium*, which has silver and green foliage that persists for many months. Tulips are rarely thought of as foliage plants, but some have leaves with wavy margins; others are mottled, and a few have truly variegated leaves. The dahlia

'Bishop of Llandaff' has a very dramatic growth of black-red foliage before and as the bright red blooms appear.

Other bulbs produce much taller leaves that are either rigid structures, as in the crocosmias and gladioli, or have a symmetrical arrangement along the stem, as seen in some lilies and fritillaries. The planting of these taller bulbs adds dramatic structure to a border, but you do need to consider their ultimate height.

BLADES OF GREEN
The swordlike leaves of the hybrid crocosmias are very attractive and last well into autumn.

FOLIAGE BULBS

Canna (all)
Cardiocrinum giganteum
Erythronium californicum
Erythronium dens-canis
Erythronium revolutum
Fritillaria imperialis
 (all)
Iris bucharica
Lilium martagon
Lilium speciosum
Lilium superbum
Tulipa kaufmanniana Group
Tulipa kolpakowskiana
Tulipa praestans 'Unicum'
 (has variegated leaves)

◄ SPIKY GREEN LEAVES
There is a special lushness given to the border by the stately habit of the Crown Imperial fritillaries.

▼ LEAFY COMBINATION
Bulbs often have very attractive and variable foliage that provides a complementary foil for their flowers.

Cannas, although tender, have large paddle-shaped leaves on a scale befitting their size, and look good as a centerpiece for seasonal bedding or in large containers. Better planted in large numbers are lilies, whose architectural leaves make an impact in the middle of a border before the flowers open.

Last there is the spring foliage of autumn-flowering bulbs. Some gardeners complain of the exuberant extent of the leaves, but strong leaf growth means prolific flowering later, so enjoy the glossy leaves of colchicums, nerines, and amaryllis throughout mid- and late spring. It is only in early summer that the leaves look unsightly, and by then other plants mask the decay. Colchicums are adaptable and can be planted among shrubs as long as some sun reaches them each day. Nerines and amaryllis need a sunny site and must not be hidden or they will fail to flower.

BULBS IN CONTAINERS

PLANTING BULBS IN CONTAINERS is an ideal way for gardeners with only a small amount of space to have permanent color just where it is needed and best appreciated. When they are not flowering, pots can simply be placed out of sight and the bulbs allowed to grow on. Areas as small as windowboxes can be utilized very successfully in this way as long as the bulbs can be removed with their roots intact so that they can be grown on in a reserve bed.

CONTAINER CHOICE

An amazing array of containers can be brought into use as homes for plants. One requisite for bulbs is that they must have an adequate depth: at least two or three times the bulb's own depth in planting and then the at least that depth again for root development. Also, water must be able to drain away quickly; if it does not, the situation can soon be remedied by drilling extra holes in the base of the container.

When choosing your containers, bear in mind that plastic pots are lighter than terracotta – an important consideration if you wish to move them – and their weight can be further restricted by using a layer of polystyrene pieces as drainage in the base of the pot. The thickness of the decorative pot combined with the plastic will slow down evaporation by keeping the soil cooler, thereby reducing the need to water. Use a soil-based mix and some fertilizer so that the bulbs will build up after flowering for the following year.

When the bulbs have flowered and are placed back in the garden, continue to water them and feed them with a dilute tomato-type fertilizer until the leaves begin to die down in order to aid the following year's bulb growth. If space is limited, the pots of resting bulbs can be stacked up until it's time to check the bulbs and start their growth again.

▲ HEIGHT AND STRUCTURE
Tulips provide the focal point for the display in this container, creating height and bringing color to the arrangement.

◄ FANCY FRITILLARY
Planting combinations of bulbs in containers provides pleasing color and shape. Here the highlight is Fritillaria meleagris.

FLOWERS THROUGH THE YEAR

Container gardens can challenge the grower who wants to have bulbs in flower through the year. In the early part of the year, crocuses, glory of the snow (*Chionodoxa*), grape hyacinths (*Muscari*), and snowdrops (*Galanthus*) will take you well into spring, when ipheions and small daffodils (*Narcissus*) come into their own. In summer, the amazing multiflora begonias give a very long-lasting display. The small onions, such as golden garlic (*Allium moly*) and nodding onion (*A. cernuum*), look lovely alongside the white flowers of *Ornithogalum nutans* and the star of Bethlehem (*O. umbellatum*). If space permits, consider any type of lily: they look good in containers, they do not take up too much space, and they look stunning as a backdrop to your display.

All cyclamens – including the slightly tender florists' cyclamens – make excellent container plants, and although they are slow-growing, they will flower while young. They are best suited to semi-shaded positions and can last for several years if repotted occasionally.

The small-flowered dahlias are hard to beat for the density of their flowers, which last from summer through to autumn; regular deadheading will encourage them to flower for longer.

Plastic pots can be placed inside more decorative pots for display

A microclimate against a wall or in an alley is surprisingly useful for protecting pots from extremes of temperature. During the winter, the common snowdrop (*Galanthus nivalis*) cultivars, *Iris reticulata*, *Crocus tommasinianus*, and *Cyclamen coum* can bring color to the dullest day.

BULBS FOR POTS

Colchicum tenorei
Crocus tommasinianus
 f. *albus*
Crocus tommasinianus
 'Ruby Giant'
Cyclamen coum
Dahlia 'Fascination'
Dahlia 'Preston Park'
Galanthus nivalis
 (all)
Hyacinthus orientalis
 (all)
Iris 'Harmony'
Iris 'Katharine Hodgkin'
Nerine undulata

POTTED DAHLIAS
*Late in the season, dahlias
can be placed against a
background of foliage to
enliven a border.*

BULB CONTAINERS IN BORDERS

A USEFUL METHOD FOR MAKING A BORDER PERFORM CONSISTENTLY throughout the year is to introduce bulbs, by way of containers, into spaces that would otherwise lack interest once the first flush of spring has passed. This method of bringing instant color to an area can be done simply by placing or burying containers in the border at a chosen spot. The use of such pots will, however, need careful consideration as to their color, size, and stability.

FILLING SEASONAL GAPS

To make a feature of these introductions quite large pots will be required, especially for bigger species. The moveable bulb pots need not be attractive if they are to be buried, so plastic is quite adequate. The plants will need a nursery in which to spend most of the year, where they are watered and fed to prepare them for their big moment. Alternatively, some gardeners grow the bulbs in lattice pond baskets sunk in the ground and then move them to their required location (*see p.53*). This is a useful method for spring-flowering bulbs, which tend to be shorter, and has the advantage of leaving the roots free to grow once they extend beyond the basket, thereby reducing the need for watering.

SUITING BULBS TO CONTAINERS

Your chosen bulbs should be planted up in a good-quality soil-based potting mix. Container cultivation allows you the opportunity to grow any bulb you like by carefully matching the type of mix to the requirements of the bulb. Most bulbous plants prefer soil that is neutral or alkaline, but there are a few – often the woodlanders, for example, some lilies and their relatives – that prefer acidic conditions. *Lilium speciosum* and the American turkscap lily (*L. superbum*) require an acidic potting mix if they are to grow well. This mix generally dries out more quickly than the soil-based type, and the bulbs will need supplemental feeding throughout the growing season.

POTS OF BEGONIAS
Watering and feeding can keep these buried containers of begonias flowering for longer than those grown in the open border.

GOOD GAP FILLERS

Camassia cusickii
Camassia leichtlinii
Canna 'Assaut'
Canna 'President'
Canna 'Wyoming'
Eucomis bicolor
Gladiolus (all)
Lilium superbum
Lilium speciosum var. *rubrum*
Tulipa (all)

◀ LILIES IN A BORDER.
*Lilies are among the best
subjects for burying in a
border. Lilies can be grown in
pots in a separate area before
being planted out in summer.*

▼ SURFACE CONTAINER
*Tulips are ideally suited to
growing in containers and
bring a short term, but very
welcome, burst of color to
the border in spring.*

CONTAINER CHOICE

If you use plastic containers, make sure that
they are free of deep folds or creases, since
such indentations can attract slugs and
snails that, in turn, may devour the
bulb foliage and ruin all your careful
preparation. An old bucket, especially a
smooth-sided, metal one, makes an
excellent subterranean planter. Drill holes
in the base of the bucket for drainage.

> Tall plants in containers
> will benefit from
> some support

Whatever the container, if the plants are
tall it is good practice to insert discreet
supports before the bulbs grow and need
staking. In borders, the taller the bulb, the
greater the impact, especially in summer,
when the perennial plants will be at their
maximum height. White-flowered bulbs,
such as galtonias and some lilies, look
stunning against a background of dark,
shady foliage. Red and orange bulbs are set
off very well against gray foliage plants.

Pots of taller bulbs need to be anchored to
the ground, since wind can wreck a display.
Heavy wire bent into hooks, with one end
pushed well into the ground, is an effective
anchor and can easily be hidden.
Alternatively, use large stones as topdressing. A group of containers can be
lashed together, or linked by heavy-guage
wire bent to resemble paper clips.

The last consideration is moving large,
moist pots. Lifting is risky, so a sack
barrow (like a porter's trolley) is essential
for safe movement through the garden.

USING BULBS FOR FRAGRANCE

THE SCENT FROM FLOWERS – including bulbs – is one of their main attractions and can be delightful on a still day at any time of the year. In winter, scent is harder to detect, since either the flowers do not release their perfumes so readily or the atmosphere inhibits their upward movement. If the individual flowers of some snowdrops (*Galanthus*) are picked and brought into a warm room, however, then the appealing scents can be detected.

GARDEN SCENT

The use of raised beds as a method of bulb and small plant cultivation is desirable for many reasons. The fact that the flowers are nearer to the admirer is one, because this proximity also brings their fragrance closer, which is particularly useful; many sweetly scented bulbs are quite small. Even without a raised bed, it is a good idea to consider planting scented bulbs close to doors and along pathways, where their perfumes can be regularly enjoyed.

Some bulbs are very fragrant – a planting of English bluebells in mid-spring, for example, is full of the flowers' wonderfully sweet smell. In contrast, ramsons (*Allium ursinum*) can fill a damp woodland with a pungent garlic odor, especially if the leaves are crushed. Most scents are far more subtle, and it is not until you take home

Bringing bulbous flowers into the home releases their fragrances

a bunch of flowers in your car that you realize some have a special fragrance; indeed, the scent of jonquils (*Narcissus jonquilla*) can be quite overpowering in a confined space.

LILY FRAGRANCE
Lilies are renowned for their fragrance. Be careful of the pollen when close to the flowers, because it can stain clothing.

FRAGRANT BULBS

Crocus (many)
Gladiolus tristis
Hyacinthoides non-scripta
Hyacinthus orientalis
(all)
Iris 'Cantab'
Iris 'Joyce'
Muscari macrocarpum
Tulipa (many)

HEADY HYACINTHS
*The scent from hyacinths is
particularly noticeable on
a warm day.*

Bulb scents are not very well documented, so you may want to keep scent notes of your own. When your bulbs are in flower for the first time, try to place the smell. It may not always be a pleasant one. Some bulbs, such as the fritillaries, have a chemical smell like household bleach, while the crown imperial (*Fritillaria imperialis*) emits a skunky scent when either its leaves are crushed or its bulb damaged.

During warm, still, summer evenings daytime scents will mingle with those released at night. The perfumes of other plants, such as honeysuckle (*Lonicera*) and night-scented stocks (*Matthiola*), are joined at these times by those of the little cream *Gladiolus tristis*, which, like the others, attempts to attract moths as pollinators.

FRAGRANT BULBS INDOORS

Having bulbous flowers in the house or greenhouse, either as cut flowers or grown in pots, brings their fragrances into a confined space for all to enjoy. Hyacinths,

for example, have a heady perfume that will fill a room for days. As cut stems, the range of scents from bulbs is much greater than expected. The grape hyacinths (*Muscari*) are very refreshing, tulips can be quite spicy, and many cyclamens are very sweetly scented. Experiment by picking different flowers; those from the colder months may well surprise you by their unexpected release of perfume in the warmer atmosphere, often undetected when the flowers bloom outside.

SCENTED DAFFODILS
Some daffodils, such as Narcissus 'Pipit', *have
a lovely, delicate scent. This is a bonus worth
checking when you are buying new bulbs.*

NATURALIZING BULBS

To SEE BULBS NATURALIZED in grassland or light woodland is one of the more breathtaking sights. It does not need to be on a grand scale, but the effect can be copied in miniature around any deciduous tree. Wherever your site, you can find a small space for such a planting, but look first at nearby gardens and woodlands to see what thrives locally, then start with these bulbs. When your bulbs start to set seeds you will know that they are doing well.

PREPARATION

Naturalizing bulbs needs some preparation to ensure success. First, any taprooted plants such as dandelions need to be removed from the area you intend to use and the grass cut prior to planting in autumn. If you are planting a small area, then the flowering heights of your selected bulbs require sorting so that the smaller species are not smothered by, for example, floppy daffodil (*Narcissus*) foliage. Normally, however, random planting looks the most natural, and to achieve this some people advocate gently throwing the bulbs into the site and then planting them where they fall. A bulb planter, is useful, although for large-scale planting insert a spade and wiggle it back and forth to make a slit for the bulb. Repair the hole with your boot (*see p.51*).

In woodland settings, which can mean a single deciduous tree but usually refers to a shady place where grass does not thrive, any grass that is present will need to be removed before planting. You are restricted to shade-loving woodland bulbs, which flower before the tree canopy fills out.

BULB CHOICE

Next comes the pleasant task of choosing your bulbs. This selection has a very restful and quiet charm: Lent lily (*Narcissus pseudonarcissus*), snake's head fritillary (*Fritillaria meleagris*), common snowdrop

BLUEBELL CARPET
A bluebell wood in spring is a magnificent sight and, en masse, *emits an attractive scent. Many of these sites are now protected by law from any disturbance.*

NATURAL SETTING

GRASSLAND
Colchicum (all species)
Fritillaria meleagris
Galanthus (all species)
Leucojum aestivum
Leucojum vernum
Narcissus (all)
Ornithogalum (all species)

WOODLAND
Anemone nemorosa
Cyclamen coum
Cyclamen hederifolium
Galanthus (all species)
Hyacinthoides hispanica
Hyacinthoides non-scripta
Lilium (all)
Muscari (all species)
Scilla (all species)

▲ DAFFODIL WOOD
Daffodils look their best in light woodland and open meadows, mimicking the habits of nature.

▶ SPRING MEADOW
A mixed planting of different bulbs looks beautiful in spring. The grass can be cut in summer without damaging the bulbs.

(*Galanthus nivalis*), and a hardy terrestrial orchid such as the green-winged orchid (*Orchis morio*). For more color, try introducing scillas, tulips, crocuses, ornithogalums, winter aconites (*Eranthis*), and snowflakes (*Leucojum*). For a naturalized autumn planting, consider *Colchicum autumnale*, the autumn crocus (*Crocus nudiflorus*), *C. ochroleucus*, *C. speciosus*, and *C. medius*, all of which will thrive in short grass.

In the woodland garden there is an opportunity to experiment with many of the shade-loving bulbs from around the world, but do remember that it is not appropriate to naturalize exotic bulbs in native woodland unless it is an extension of your garden. Lilies thrive in a large space and look very natural. Selections have been made from the little wood anemone (*Anemone nemorosa*), so that a range of darker shades is now available, and there are double selections available to decorate the woodland floor. Many of the scillas and grape hyacinths (*Muscari*) also look very natural in woodland settings and are best grown in drifts to create a stunning effect. The colony will soon start to spread by self-sowing and will in time take on a natural, wild appearance.

BULBS FOR COLOR

THE USE OF COLOR in the garden needs to be planned and its effects understood. Using colors from opposing segments of the color wheel will produce the most dramatic effects. Choosing colors from adjacent segments will produce more subtle combinations. Walk around local parks or public gardens for your initial inspiration for planting.

COLOR WHEEL

USING HOT COLORS

Hot colors are those at the red end of the spectrum. They are intense and vibrant and seem to shorten the border by appearing to be closer to you than they really are. The use of bulbs with bold and lance-shaped leaves can mute the effect of hot colors and add to the "tropical" feeling. Such a border is usually best suited to a sunny position and is generally planted alongside herbaceous plants, where the bulbs soon provide height and dramatic color. The bulbs are best planted in solid blocks of color rather than separated out as individual bright spots.

The hot colors are found mainly in late spring- and summer-flowering bulbs, which in turn are usually medium to tall in stature. Tulips, crocosmias, cannas, and some anemones can provide an eye-catching display. The farther south the garden, the stronger the sunlight, so more fiery colors will seem less strident in Florida than in Maine; conversely, pastel shades appear washed out in bright sun but look vibrant in more northern gardens. Try different plantings if the colors prove to be too strong or are not to your liking. In an emergency, bulbs can be moved any time the ground is not frozen, and although they may not flower the following year, they will survive.

SUNNY YELLOWS
A block of a strong color such as yellow needs careful consideration but can produce a stunning effect.

FIERY BULBS

Anemone × fulgens	Dahlia 'Doris Day'
Anemone pavonina	Dahlia 'Murillo'
Canna 'Assaut'	Lilium pomponium
Canna 'King Midas'	Lilium pumilium
Crocosmia × crocosmiiflora 'Emily Mckenzie'	Tulipa 'Apeldoorn'
	Tulipa 'Apeldoorn's Elite'
Crocosmia × crocosmiiflora 'Star of the East'	Tulipa linifolia
	Tulipa 'Orange Bouquet'
Crocosmia latifolia 'Lucifer'	Tulipa praestans 'Fusilier'
Dahlia 'Bishop of Llandaff'	Tulipa 'Red Riding Hood'

◄ RED AND PINK
The strong reds of crocosmias can be muted by the planting of an appropriate pink shade, such as that of the verbena shown here.

▼ A TAPESTRY OF ORANGE
When planning a pattern of colors such as this one, always make sure that the flowering periods of the different plants are going to coincide.

USING COOL COLORS

The English garden is renowned for its use of cool colors, which suit the climate and light intensity very well. Working with nature, bulbs can be used to enhance a border or an arrangement of patio containers for all four seasons. Here, white, pale blue, pink, and pale primrose can make a very restful and beautiful display.

In winter, bulbs often reign supreme in providing early color, when the snowdrop (*Galanthus*) and the white and pale pink forms of *Cyclamen coum* create a very cool

---

Cooler colors are best suited to regions with a lower light intensity

---

background during the shortest days of the year. As spring develops, the choice becomes immense from the white and pale forms of scillas, grape hyacinths (*Muscari*), dog's-tooth violets (*Erythronium*), crocuses, daffodils (*Narcissus*), and puschkinias. These bulbs are best when interspersed between plants such as lungwort (*Pulmonaria*) and Christmas roses

(*Helleborus niger*), and small shrubs such as *Daphne mezereum* f. *alba*. For pale primrose, *Fritillaria pallidiflora* has large, pendent bells surrounded by elongate leaves. The white snakeshead fritillary is one of the most beautiful bulbs when seen scattered throughout a spring planting.

During summer, the garden can be a refreshing place, especially on hot days, when the illusion of coolness is very welcome. At this time, the border will benefit from a mixture of herbaceous plants used as a backdrop for the transient bulbs. Holding its own with any is the stately giant lily (*Cardiocrinum giganteum*), with stout stems to more than 6ft (2m), topped by large, fragrant, trumpet-shaped flowers.

The white-flowered pompon alliums take up very little space, with their leafless stems topped by a cluster of white flowers. Other, usually medium to tall, bulbs suitable for a summer planting are ornithogalums, camassias, galtonias, snowflakes (*Leucojum*), and lilies.

There are many famous white gardens that always look their best in summer. There, new planting ideas are tried and tested regularly, so take a look at some of them for inspiration. Emulate the designs

MUSCARI BLUES
Grape hyacinth bulbs need planting very close together to obtain this dense highlight in a spring border. There are abundant leaves which, later, make an excellent weed-suppressing groundcover.

COOL BULBS

Allium 'Mount Everest'
Camassia cusickii
Crocus sieberi 'Albus'
Cyclamen hederifolium
  f. *albiflorum*
Galanthus plicatus
Galtonia candicans
Narcissus 'Thalia'
Ornithogalum narbonense
Ornithogalum nutans
Tulipa 'Purissima'

◄ COOL AND FRESH
By mixing colors, in this case pink and blue Spanish bluebells, a tapestry of pastel shades serves to highlight the fresh green leaves of a maple.

▼ BLUE SHADES OF AUTUMN
A true autumn crocus, Crocus speciosus *'Oxonian', flowers without leaves and is quite able to thrive in either sun or light shade.*

you find appealing, for very little is really new and there is no patent to a design or combination of plants.

In autumn, the light – slanting, and often hazy – is one of the attractions of the darkening year, so the planting of cool bulbs needs to reflect the muted tones of yellowing and decay. Try one of the most attractive and graceful bulbs of the entire flowering year, *Colchicum speciosum* 'Album', a thick milky-white goblet of a flower on a lime-green stem. Like most autumn colchicums, it flowers without the surprisingly large leaves, which do not begin to grow until the following spring. Another classy and classic autumn plant is the white form of the usually pink *Cyclamen hederifolium*.

FORM AND STRUCTURE

BULBS BRING RELIABLE and regular form to borders and containers. Shrubs and trees may take time to mature and produce the desired effects. Bulbs, however, flower in the season following purchase and never increase in height as the years pass. They may spread naturally, but to combat this (if it is not a characteristic you want to encourage) you face only the relatively easy task of lifting and replanting as many as you want during the resting period.

SEASONAL STRUCTURE

In contrast to the relatively short stature of winter and early spring bulbs, the species that flower later in the year are often taller and show greater diversity of color and flower shape. The leaves of the later bulbs often have a most attractive shape, texture, and color. For months after their flower stems have coiled and seed has been set, two cyclamens, *Cyclamen coum* and *C. hederifolium*, have attractive foliage that can become so dense over the years that it precludes weeds and forms a substantial groundcover. The cyclamens' leaf color varies from all green to green with silver markings to all silver. Tempting as it may be to have weeks of flowers in autumn followed by more in winter and spring, do not plant these two species together, because *C. hederifolium* will overwhelm *C. coum* with its luxuriant leaves.

> Bulbous plants provide strong vertical lines within a border

The fresh leaves of most of the dog's-tooth violets (*Erythronium*) are beautifully mottled with silver or chocolate brown, similar to those of some Greigii tulips, such

STRUCTURAL ALLIUMS
Alliums are unique in that they provide these spheres of color in the summer border and later architectural shape in the autumn. They love a sunny site and are sturdy plants that never need staking.

STATELY CANNAS
*Strong shape and color
are provided by cannas.
Although tender, they grow
very quickly in spring to
provide an attractive centerpiece to a summer border.*

STRUCTURE BULBS

Allium cristophii
Allium hollandicum
Cardiocrinum giganteum
Crocosmia (all)
Fritillaria imperialis
Lilium martagon
Lilium superbum

as 'Red Riding Hood'. When thinking
of foliage, consider the shape, clusters,
and sheen of fresh leaves, since these
characteristics all add an extra dimension
to plants we usually consider simply for
their flowers. Equally, remember that
flower stems are quite bare and may form
strong vertical features in the garden long
after the flowers have faded. Alliums, some
fritillaries, and the giant cardiocrinum lily
are all attractive in this respect.

The impact of the display in its entirety
should also be considered at the time of
planting. The ultimate height and spread of
the plants need to be established, as well as
the visual impact of the garden in other
seasons. The shape created by the planting

may be thin and winding, or a wide plot
of densely planted bulbs designed to make
a focal point of color. Large bulbs, such
as cannas, lilies, and fritillaries, are bold
enough in their own right to be used as
individual plants in a mixed border,
flowering and then becoming submerged
by summer foliage.

The popularity of formal structure
provided by a tightly clipped boxwood
hedge is growing. This planting is usually
in some form of geometrical pattern within
which bulbs are planted to give blocks of
contrasting color or height and shape.
The size of hedge needs to be considered
when planting short bulbs such as muscari,
hyacinths, and narcissus (*see p.44–45*).

PLANTING PLANS FOR BULBS

CHOOSING A PLANTING STYLE

THE VERSATILITY OF BULBS means that they can give new gardens an air of maturity within a single year, while in more established gardens they provide an almost instant fillip of color or shape where it is needed. The plans shown here not only cover the traditional use of bulbs in spring but also give further ideas for summer- and autumn-flowering bulbs, often rather neglected. Whatever your choice of season, bulbs can create the desired impact of color or design.

CHANGES IN GARDEN DESIGN

Gardening trends are constantly evolving. The introduction of new bulbs and the development of micropropagation has given the gardener a far greater choice at an affordable price. For instance, a few years ago, a single bulb of the beautiful *Crocus sieberi* 'Albus' was prohibitively expensive. Now it is so modestly priced that it is available in many plant retail outlets. For the avant-garde, major flower shows create great excitement with their innovative ideas on design and planting. Bulbs often play their part, being used as architectural features and in specific color blocks and bands to lead the eye through a display. The amateur gardener can copy elements of these ideas and incorporate them into most garden situations, and the new plants can be acquired as they inevitably become more readily available.

VIBRANT COLOR *The orange-yellow lily* (Lilium pyrenaicum) *and the herbaceous pea* (Lathyrus aureus) *contrast with the dense blue flowers of the shrubby evergreen ceanothus. The lily and the pea are grown on the north side of the shrub so that their colorful display lasts longer and is not bleached by the sun.*

◄ ALLIUM ALL-STARS *Mixed alliums are attractively set off by the purple foliage of heucheras.*

A Spring Border

A border planted to be at its peak in spring is one of the highlights of the garden. Here the traditional bulbs have been interspersed with mostly shrubby plants, which will add to the show and provide some year-round interest.

Herbaceous plants, such as hostas and grasses, can be planted to provide cover for any bare patches of soil that appear once the bulb foliage begins to turn yellow and die down later in the growing season.

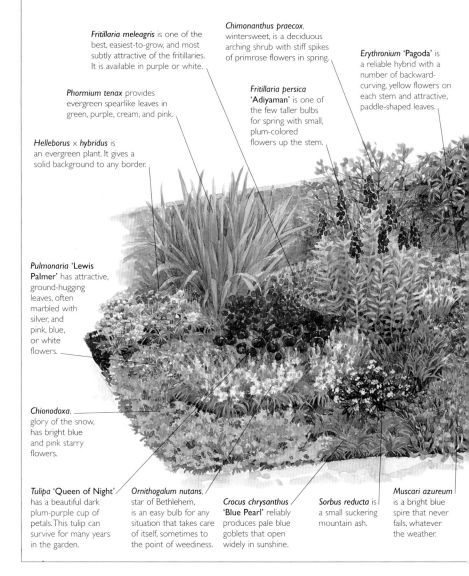

Fritillaria meleagris is one of the best, easiest-to-grow, and most subtly attractive of the fritillaries. It is available in purple or white.

Chimonanthus praecox, wintersweet, is a deciduous arching shrub with stiff spikes of primrose flowers in spring.

Erythronium 'Pagoda' is a reliable hybrid with a number of backward-curving, yellow flowers on each stem and attractive, paddle-shaped leaves.

Phormium tenax provides evergreen spearlike leaves in green, purple, cream, and pink.

Fritillaria persica 'Adiyaman' is one of the few taller bulbs for spring with small, plum-colored flowers up the stem.

Helleborus × hybridus is an evergreen plant. It gives a solid background to any border.

Pulmonaria 'Lewis Palmer' has attractive, ground-hugging leaves, often marbled with silver, and pink, blue, or white flowers.

Chionodoxa, glory of the snow, has bright blue and pink starry flowers.

Tulipa 'Queen of Night' has a beautiful dark plum-purple cup of petals. This tulip can survive for many years in the garden.

Ornithogalum nutans, star of Bethlehem, is an easy bulb for any situation that takes care of itself, sometimes to the point of weediness.

Crocus chrysanthus 'Blue Pearl' reliably produces pale blue goblets that open widely in sunshine.

Sorbus reducta is a small suckering mountain ash.

Muscari azureum is a bright blue spire that never fails, whatever the weather.

PLANTING PLAN

1 *Helleborus* × *hybridus*, 18in (45cm) tall
2 *Pulmonaria* 'Lewis Palmer', 14in (35cm) tall
3 *Phormium tenax*, 12ft (4m) tall
4 *Tulipa* 'Queen of Night', 24in (60cm) tall
5 *Fritillaria meleagris*, 12in (30cm) tall
6 *Fritillaria persica* 'Adiyaman', 5ft (1.5m) tall
7 *Chimonanthus praecox*, 12ft (4m) tall
8 *Erythronium* 'Pagoda', 6–14in (15–35cm) tall
9 *Sarcococca confusa*, 6ft (2m) tall
10 *Narcissus* 'Thalia', 14in (35cm) tall
11 *Chionodoxa luciliae*, 6in (15cm) tall
12 *Ornithogalum nutans*, 8–24in (20–60cm) tall
13 *Crocus chrysanthus* 'Blue Pearl', 3in (7cm) tall
14 *Sorbus reducta*, 3–5ft (1–1.5m) tall
15 *Galanthus plicatus* subsp. *byzantinus*,
     8in (20cm) tall
16 *Tulipa praestans* 'Fusilier', 12in (30cm) tall
17 *Iris reticulata* 'J.S. Dijt', 4–6in (10–15cm) tall
18 *Oxalis adenophylla*, 4in (10cm) tall
19 *Iris* 'Harmony', 4–6in (10–15cm) tall
20 *Muscari azureum*, 4in (10cm) tall
21 *Daphne alpina*, 24in (60cm) tall
22 *Erythronium dens-canis*, 4–6in (10–15cm) tall

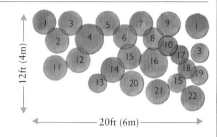

12ft (4m)

20ft (6m)

MORE CHOICES

TALL (over 36in/90cm)
Fritillaria imperialis
  cultivars

MEDIUM
(12–36in/30–90cm)
Narcissus 'February Gold'
Narcissus 'Jetfire'
Tulipa 'Queen of Sheba'

SMALL
(below 12in/30cm)
Muscari latifolium
Narcissus 'Jack Snipe'
Scilla bifolia

Sarcococca confusa is a
small evergreen bush
with scented flowers.

Narcissus 'Thalia' is a pale
beauty of excellent stature
and garden worthiness that
will give years of pleasure.

Iris reticulata 'J.S. Dijt'
is very reliable for
cold areas. It has
purple flowers in
early spring.

Oxalis adenophylla
is a tiny South American
plant, that is not at all
invasive. It is best grown
in a sunny site.

ERYTHRONIUM
DENS-CANIS
*This is the only
European member of
this genus. The leaves
alone make a very
attractive groundcover.*

Tulipa praestans
'Fusilier' is a stunning
Asian beauty with a
number of very
bright red flowers
per stem.

Daphne alpina
is a deciduous
shrub that has
scented, white
flowers.

Galanthus plicatus
subsp. byzantinus
is a fine, broad-leaved
snowdrop, which
grows well in sun
or shade.

Iris 'Harmony',
although early into
flower, will withstand
the worst of any
weather and continue
to bloom.

A SUMMER BORDER

This summer border is one in which bulbs predominate but have the support of other herbaceous and woody plants to provide the interest in the bed at other times of the year. The dark background of a yew hedge helps set off the display. Summer bulbs are often tall and slim, taking little horizontal space, and this enables the gardener with a small space to grow an interesting range while avoiding undue overcrowding.

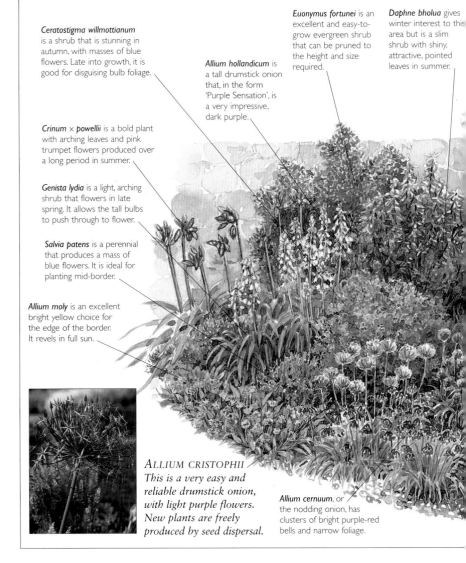

Ceratostigma willmottianum is a shrub that is stunning in autumn, with masses of blue flowers. Late into growth, it is good for disguising bulb foliage.

Allium hollandicum is a tall drumstick onion that, in the form 'Purple Sensation', is a very impressive, dark purple.

Euonymus fortunei is an excellent and easy-to-grow evergreen shrub that can be pruned to the height and size required.

Daphne bholua gives winter interest to this area but is a slim shrub with shiny, attractive, pointed leaves in summer.

Crinum × *powellii* is a bold plant with arching leaves and pink trumpet flowers produced over a long period in summer.

Genista lydia is a light, arching shrub that flowers in late spring. It allows the tall bulbs to push through to flower.

Salvia patens is a perennial that produces a mass of blue flowers. It is ideal for planting mid-border.

Allium moly is an excellent bright yellow choice for the edge of the border. It revels in full sun.

ALLIUM CRISTOPHII
This is a very easy and reliable drumstick onion, with light purple flowers. New plants are freely produced by seed dispersal.

Allium cernuum, or the nodding onion, has clusters of bright purple-red bells and narrow foliage.

PLANTING PLAN

1 *Crinum × powellii*, up to 5ft (1.5m) tall
2 *Genista lydia*, 24in (60cm) tall
3 *Galtonia candicans*, 3–4ft (1–1.2m) tall
4 *Allium hollandicum*, 3ft (1m) tall
5 *Euonymus fortunei*, 24in (60cm) tall
6 *Daphne bholua*, 6–12ft (2–4m) tall
7 *Cardiocrinum giganteum*, 5–12ft (1.5–4m) tall
8 *Camassia cusickii*, 24–32in (60–80cm) tall
9 *Allium moly*, 6–10in (15–25cm) tall
10 *Salvia patens*, 18–24in (45–60cm) tall
11 *Ceratostigma willmottianum*, 3ft (1m) tall
12 *Allium cristophii*, 12–24in (30–60cm) tall
13 *Crocosmia × crocosmiiflora* 'Dusky Maiden',
   24–36in (60–90cm) tall
14 *Allium cernuum*, 12–24in (30–60cm) tall
15 *Callistephus chinensis* Milady Mixed, 12in (30cm) tall
16 *Sedum spectabile*, 24in (60cm) tall
17 *Taxus baccata*, 30ft (10m) tall if unpruned

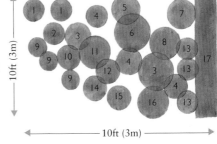

10ft (3m)

10ft (3m)

MORE CHOICES

TALL (over 36in/90cm)
Crocosmia 'Lucifer'
Lilium martagon
Lilium regale

MEDIUM
(12–36in/30–90cm)
Gladiolus communis subsp.
  byzantinus
Lilium 'Red Night'
Ornithogalum pyrenaicum

SMALL (below 12in/30cm)
Allium insubricum
Allium orophilum

Cardiocrinum giganteum
is the most dramatic of all
summer-flowering bulbs.
Grow a number together so
that at least one or two are
in flower each year.

Taxus baccata or other yew
hedges make an excellent
backdrop to any border and
are very easily controlled to
suit the height and width
requirements of the display.

Camassia cusickii can be
accommodated throughout
the border and will
propagate itself
by seed dispersal.

Galtonia candicans is often called
the summer hyacinth. This graceful,
white-flowered bulb flowers for a
rather long period.

Crocosmia × crocosmiiflora 'Dusky
Maiden' has beautiful, dark foliage
and orange flowers. It tends to be
shorter in full sun.

Callistephus chinensis Milady Mixed,
China aster, is a short-growing annual
with double, aster-like flowers in a range
of colors. It is tolerant of drought.

Sedum spectabile is a late summer-
flowering perennial with attractive
leaves and large, flat flowerheads
that attract bees.

AN AUTUMN BORDER

An attractive, almost unexpected, bonus of the autumn bulb border is the introduction of fresh flowers it brings to the waning garden. Small spring- and summer-flowering shrubs can be planted with the bulbs to bring greater interest to the border in late autumn. A number of bulbs have attractive spring foliage, especially the cyclamen, with its silver-veined, ivylike leaves that provide a dense ground-cover for many months.

PLANTING PLAN

 1 *Amaryllis belladonna*, 24in (60cm) tall
 2 *Crocus speciosus* 'Oxonian', 4–6in (10–15cm) tall
 3 *Colchicum speciosum* 'Album', 7in (18cm) tall
 4 *Festuca glauca*, 12in (30cm) tall
 5 *Perovskia* 'Blue Spire', 4ft (1.2m) tall
 6 *Sternbergia lutea*, 6in (15cm) tall
 7 *Colchicum* 'Waterlily', 5in (12cm) tall
 8 *Cyclamen hederifolium*, 4–5in (10–13cm) tall
 9 *Eucomis bicolor*, 12–24in (30–60cm) tall
10 *Nerine bowdenii*, 18in (45cm) tall

10ft (3m)

12ft (4m)

Perovskia **'Blue Spire'** should be pruned back to a framework each spring to encourage a compact and free-flowering shrub for the autumn.

Colchicum speciosum **'Album'** has beautiful, goblet-shaped white flowers. It grows best in sun, and well-drained enriched soil.

COLCHICUM 'WATERLILY'
This prolific grower makes a mound of multipetalled flowers of strident pink. It blooms later in the season.

MORE CHOICES

TALL
(over 36in/90cm)
Eucomis pole-evansii
Lilium formosanum
Lilium speciosum var. *rubrum*

MEDIUM
(12–36in/30–90cm)
Colchicum 'Pink Goblet'

Colchicum speciosum
Nerine bowdenii 'Alba'

SMALL
(below 12in/30cm)
Crocus kotschyanus
Crocus ochroleucus
Cyclamen cilicium

AMARYLLIS BELLADONNA
Tall stems are topped with
funnels of pink that seem to
be triggered into flowering
by heavy rain in late
summer.

Nerine bowdenii
flowers best in dry,
sunny spots that
are shunned by
other plants.

STERNBERGIA LUTEA
These goblets are strong
yellow, which is quite an
unusual color for an autumn
bulb. Thrives in full sun.

Eucomis bicolor is a large South
African bulb that flowers in late
summer. It grows best in well-
fertilized soil in full sun. It has
quite attractive seed capsules,
which can be removed if seed
is not required.

Crocus speciosus 'Oxonian' is a dark
violet crocus best planted close
together in groups or drifts.

Festuca glauca is an attractive,
evergreen grass that is easily
grown and never becomes a
nuisance by seeding or running.

Cyclamen hederifolium
comes from around the
Mediterranean, but is totally
hardy and at home in
temperate gardens.

A WINTER BORDER

There is a surprisingly wide range of winter-flowering bulbs to be considered. An island bed such as this is best positioned close to a paved walkway for easy access in wintry weather. The structure provided by deciduous shrubs and small trees is ideal because it provides shade for the bulbs when they are dormant. The shrubs also provide an attractive and natural background for the delicate-looking woodland and meadow bulbs.

MORE CHOICES

MEDIUM
(12–36in/30–90cm)
Narcissus 'Rijnveld's Early Sensation'

SMALL
(below 12in/30cm)
Corydalis malkensis

Crocus sieberi 'Albus'
  C. *sieberi* 'Violet Queen'
Galanthus elwesii
  G. 'Magnet'
  G. *nivalis*
  G. *plicatus*

Acer davidii, snakebark maple, is a small deciduous tree ideally suited to smaller gardens, with the bonus of attractive bark.

LEUCOJUM VERNUM
The snowflakes are taller and larger than snowdrops but equally attractive and easy to establish.

Philadelphus coronarius is a shrub that has scented white flowers in summer. It can be pruned annually to keep an attractive framework.

Eranthis hyemalis, or winter aconite, quickly opens as the days lengthen. Each flower is framed by a ruff of leaves.

PLANTING PLAN

1 *Galanthus plicatus* subsp. *byzantinus*,
  8in (20cm) tall
2 *Leucojum vernum*, 8–12in (20–30cm) tall
3 *Acer davidii*, 50ft (15m) tall
4 *Hamamelis mollis*, 12ft (4m) tall
5 *Philadelphus coronarius*, 10ft (3m) tall
6 *Eranthis hyemalis*, 2–3in (5–8cm) tall
7 *Scilla bifolia*, 3–6in (8–15cm) tall
8 *Cyclamen coum*, 2–3in (5–8cm) tall

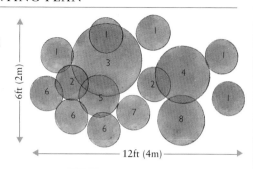

6ft (2m)

12ft (4m)

Hamamelis mollis, or witch hazel, has extraordinarily fragrant flowers borne in late winter on leafless branches. They add much to any winter bed.

CYCLAMEN COUM
Short and hardy, these maroon, pink, or white flowers shine during the dull winter days. The leaves vary from plain green to the near silver leaves of the Pewter Group.

Galanthus plicatus subsp. *byzantinus* is an early-flowering form of this variable and bold snowdrop. It has much larger leaves than the common snowdrop *G. nivalis*.

Scilla bifolia will seed around to form a beautiful blue carpet of starry bells.

A Layered Border

This is a border where the use of bulbs means that color and shape can be achieved from winter through late spring. The border rises in height as the seasons progress, with the earlier-flowering bulbs hidden by the taller spring flowers. Once late spring arrives, the border will need to be cleared of foliage and neatened to allow late perennials and a few colorful annuals to provide the summer and autumn interest.

MORE CHOICES

TALL (over 36in/90cm)
Allium hollandicum
Cardiocrinum giganteum
Lilium martagon

MEDIUM
(12–36in/30–90cm)
Anemone pavonina
Leucojum vernum
Tulipa praestans 'Fusilier'

SMALL (below
12in/30cm)
Galanthus elwesii
Muscari armeniacum
Narcissus 'Tête-à-tête'

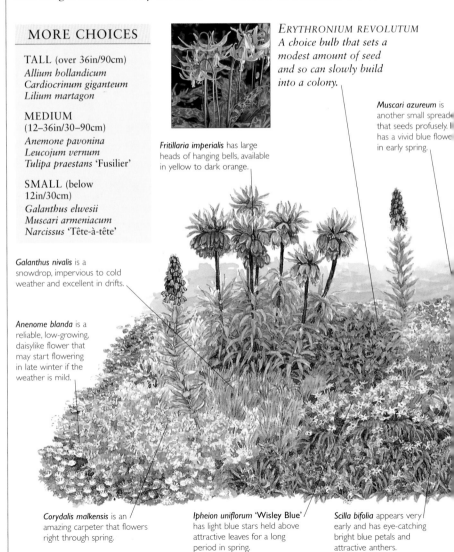

ERYTHRONIUM REVOLUTUM
A choice bulb that sets a modest amount of seed and so can slowly build into a colony.

Muscari azureum is another small spreader that seeds profusely. It has a vivid blue flower in early spring.

Fritillaria imperialis has large heads of hanging bells, available in yellow to dark orange.

Galanthus nivalis is a snowdrop, impervious to cold weather and excellent in drifts.

Anemone blanda is a reliable, low-growing, daisylike flower that may start flowering in late winter if the weather is mild.

Corydalis malkensis is an amazing carpeter that flowers right through spring.

Ipheion uniflorum 'Wisley Blue' has light blue stars held above attractive leaves for a long period in spring.

Scilla bifolia appears very early and has eye-catching bright blue petals and attractive anthers.

PLANTING PLAN

1 *Anemone blanda*, 6in (15cm) tall
2 *Galanthus nivalis*, 4in (10cm) tall
3 *Fritillaria imperialis*, 5ft(1.5m) tall
4 *Erythronium revolutum*, 8–12in(20–30cm) tall
5 *Corydalis solida*, 10in (25cm) tall
6 *Muscari azureum*, 4in (10cm) tall
7 *Fritillaria persica* 'Adiyaman', 5ft (1.5m) tall
8 *Tulipa linifolia* Batalini Group 14in (35cm) tall
9 *Ornithogalum nutans*, 8–24in (20–60cm) tall
10 *Corydalis malkensis*, 3–6in (8–15cm) tall
11 *Ipheion uniflorum* 'Wisley Blue', 6–8in (15–20cm) tall
12 *Scilla bifolia*, 3–6in (8–15cm) tall
13 *Anemone coronaria*, 12–18in (30–45cm) tall
14 *Iris* 'Katharine Hodgkin', 5in (12cm) tall
15 *Puschkinia scilloides*, 8in (20cm) tall

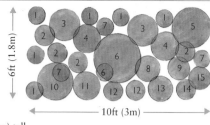

6ft (1.8m)

10ft (3m)

Tulipa linifolia
Batalini Group are
reliable tulips that
range from red
through to cream,
or a mix of both.

Fritillaria persica 'Adiyaman'
is a rather tall plant with
attractive plum-colored bells
above blue-green leaves.
It may need supporting.

IRIS 'KATHARINE HODGKIN'
*This iris is popular for its
unique colors and for its
weatherproof nature
early in the year.*

Corydalis solida is most
attractive in its red, pink,
or white forms.

Anenome coronaria flowers
very early in the year if in
full sun. It is best grown in
very fast-draining soil.

Ornithogalum nutans is almost
silvery in sunlight. This is a low-key
but attractive member of the
mostly white genus.

Puschkinia scilloides are very easy
to grow. The flowers have white
stripes on a blue background.
Grow in sun or part shade.

BULBS IN FORMAL BEDS

These small formal plantings look stunning positioned next to buildings. Any edging plants need to be naturally small. Lavender and santolina can provide a silver frame, while a small purple barberry gives a more somber edge. The hyacinth bed will need foliar feeding once the flowers fade in order to ensure good flowering the following year. Large containers, such as barrels, can be used to produce a similar effect in miniature.

PLANTING PLAN

1 *Tulipa* 'Purissima', 14in (35cm) tall
2 *Fritillaria imperialis* 'Maxima Lutea', 5ft (1.5m) tall
3 *Tulipa* 'Queen of Sheba', 24in (60cm) tall
4 *Myosotis sylvatica* 'Blue Ball', 10in (25cm) tall

6ft (2m)

6ft (2m)

Fritillaria imperialis '**Maxima Lutea**' is very impressive planted close together, with the pineapple tufts of leaves above the hanging bell flowers.

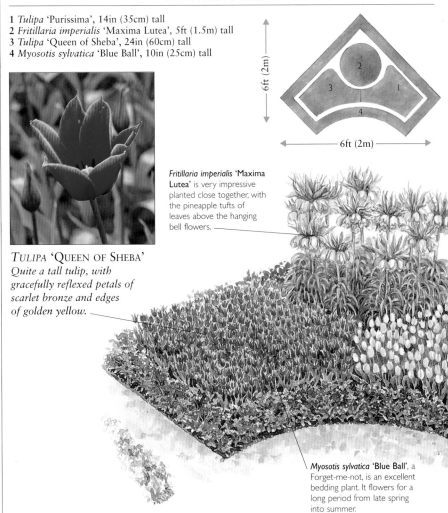

TULIPA 'QUEEN OF SHEBA'
Quite a tall tulip, with gracefully reflexed petals of scarlet bronze and edges of golden yellow.

Myosotis sylvatica '**Blue Ball**', a Forget-me-not, is an excellent bedding plant. It flowers for a long period from late spring into summer.

PLANTING PLAN

1 *Hyacinthus orientalis* 'Anna Marie', 8–12in (20–30cm) tall
2 *H. orientalis* 'Delft Blue', 8–12in (20–30cm) tall
3 *H. orientalis* 'White Pearl', 8–12in (20–30cm) tall

MORE CHOICES

SMALL (below 12in/30cm)
Hyacinthus orientalis 'Carnegie'
H. orientalis 'City of Haarlem'
H. orientalis 'L'Innocence'
H. orientalis 'Ostara'

5ft (1.5m)

5ft (1.5m)

Hyacinthus orientalis 'Delft Blue' is nearly the color of the famous china. It is a very reliable selection that is ideal for bedding.

Hyacinthus orientalis 'Anna Marie' is a light pink selection of this much beloved, fragrant flower.

Hyacinthus orientalis 'White Pearl' is used in this formal structure for the stark white needed to complete the trio.

MORE CHOICES

TALL (over 36in/90cm)
Fritillaria imperialis 'Rubra'
F. imperialis 'The Premier'

MEDIUM (12–36in/30–90cm)
Tulipa 'Golden Apeldoorn'
T. 'Queen of Night'
T. 'White Triumphator'

SMALL (below 12in/30cm)
Muscari armeniacum
Narcissus 'Tête-à-tête'

Tulipa 'Purissima' is a Fosteriana hybrid with beautiful, sturdy milk white flowers. It provides an ideal contrast to the more stridently colored varieties.

BULBS IN CONTAINERS

For small gardens, or for an area of a larger garden that is frequently used such as a patio, a display of bulbs in pots makes an eye-catching feature. The display should be in a sheltered spot, and it is wise to take some precautions against wind damage. The pots can be discreetly hooked to each other for stability, or heavy pebbles can be used as topdressing or wedged around the bases. When buying pots, look for those that have a wide base.

PLANTING PLAN

1 *Dahlias* Unwins Dwarf Group, 24in (60cm) tall
2 *Lobularia maritima*, 2–12in (5–30cm) tall
3 *Canna*, 28in (70cm) tall
4 *Galtonia candicans*, 3–4ft (1–1.2m) tall
5 *Crocosmia × crocosmiiflora* 'Gerbe d'Or',
   20in–5ft (50cm–1.5m) tall
6 *Lysimachia nummularia* 'Aurea', 2in (5cm) tall
7 *Allium moly*, 6–10in (15–25cm) tall
8 *Crocosmia × crocosmiiflora* 'Jackanapes',
   16–24in (40cm–60cm) tall
9 *Lobelia erinus* 'Cambridge Blue',
   4–9in (10–23cm) tall

6ft (1.8m)
10ft (3m)

Allium moly is a yellow-flowered onion and is very vibrant. It seeds modestly.

Crocosmia x crocosmiiflora 'Gerbe d'Or' is a very reliable plant that needs plenty of moisture and sunlight to display its best.

Dahlia Unwins Dwarf Group are ideal container plants because they will flower for a long time if deadheaded and fed.

Lobularia maritima selections are dwarf white or pale purple-pink annuals that can be sown in spring to flower that summer. Trim after flowering to encourage further flowers.

Lysimachia nummularia 'Aurea' is a very easy and reliable herbaceous perennial that has bright yellow flowers over a long period in summer.

MORE CHOICES

TALL (over 36in (90cm)
Allium hollandicum 'Purple
  Sensation'
Lilium Golden Splendor
  Group
L. speciosum var. *rubrum*

MEDIUM
(12–36in/30–90cm)
Camassia leichtlinii
  'Semiplena'
Nerine bowdenii
Tulipa linifolia

SMALL
(below 12in/30cm)
Anemone coronaria
  cultivars
Colchicum 'Waterlily'
C. speciosum 'Album'

Galtonia candicans
looks almost succulent
in growth and has
beautiful pendent bells
on a tall spire.

Cannas are stately plants,
good for the back of the
display. They will flower
for months if kept fed
and watered.

CROCOSMIA ×
CROCOSMIIFLORA
'JACKANAPES'
*This is one of the larger-
flowered hybrids. It makes
a strong statement
wherever it is grown.*

Mixed Lobelias *are*
usually used for annual
bedding or container
planting.

LOOKING AFTER YOUR BULBS

WHEN TO BUY BULBS

THE BEST TIME TO SHOP FOR BULBS is as soon as they are available in garden centers, usually from late summer onward. From late winter to early summer bulb catalogs appear, and the orders are sent out in three cycles: the first in late summer and very early autumn for autumn-flowering plants, the second from early to late autumn for spring-flowerers, and the third in spring for summer bulbs.

BUYING TIPS

The established mail-order bulb nurseries have a reputation to maintain, and usually their bulbs are of flowering size and in good condition. Other outlets may not always be as satisfactory, particularly with regard to the naming of stocks. In garden centers, the presentation of bulbs is colorful and informative, with the bulbs in aerated bags behind photographs of their flowers. Do look closely at the bulbs, because after a few weeks some may begin to deteriorate and even attempt to flower. Choosing bulbs from a basket (wearing gloves to avoid any possible irritation) is still the best and safest method of selection.

CHOOSING HEALTHY BULBS

• Always buy early and choose plump bulbs for immediate planting.
• Check the size. Undersized bulbs certainly will not flower in the first year.
• The outer tunic, or skin, should be intact and clean; it is the bulb's defense against desiccation.
• Diseased bulbs may smell unpleasant even before they show signs of deterioration.
• Reject bulbs that are in growth or have attempted to grow and then dried through lack of moisture.

Growing point should be firm

► TESTING A BULB
Gently squeeze a bulb to check that it is firm – an indication that it is healthy.

Basal plate should be firm and unblemished

▲ A GOOD BULB
The bulb should be of an even color, with no stripes or blotches, and should look healthy, without any premature leaf or root growth.

◄ LEAFY BULBS
Snowdrop and snowflake bulbs must not dry out, so they may be sold with their leaves for immediate planting.

◄ BLUEBELL WALK *A stone path, dappled in shade, winds through a sea of Spanish bluebells.*

PREPARING THE PLANTING SITE

THE VAST MAJORITY OF BULBS comes from soils that dry out to some degree during their resting period. In temperate climates, there are no regular dry periods, so to prevent the bulbs from getting too wet, you must ensure the soil is free-draining. Before planting, heavy clay soil should be deeply dug to aerate the structure and coarse sand incorporated. On sandy soils, organic matter, such as leafmold and well-rotted compost, will improve the nutrient levels.

ADDING NUTRIENTS BEFORE PLANTING

Bulbs are no different in their requirements for nutrients than other plants, but they do root in the same area just under the basal plate every year. To encourage continued flowering, nutrients can be added during a bulb's resting period. Organic material, such as compost, mushroom compost, and well-rotted manure, may be lightly forked into the bed. In a rock garden or raised bed, it may be more convenient to work in a concentrated fertilizer.

HANDLING FERTILIZER

- Always read the instructions carefully.
- Wear gloves. The latex type allow for good dexterity and are cheap enough to dispose of.
- Open and dispense in the open air to avoid breathing in any dust from the packaging.
- Dispose of empty containers or, if only part used, store in a dry, secure place.
- If mixed with water, use in a single application, because particles tend to settle.

CONCENTRATED FERTILIZERS

Organic concentrated fertilizers release nutrients slowly. These nutrients are accessible to plants as the ground warms in spring. They are best gently stirred into the soil, rather than simply scattered on top, and can be incorporated deeply at planting time. If you are concerned about the health risks of using these products, rock phosphate and seaweed meal are suitable alternatives. Inorganic fertilizers are released into the soil only once they are dissolved by either rainfall or hand watering. The pellets must not rest on any foliage, because the chemicals released soon kill any plant tissue they touch.

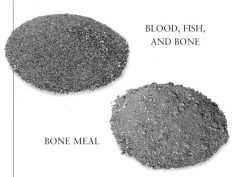

BLOOD, FISH, AND BONE

BONE MEAL

TYPES OF FERTILIZER
Always apply at the rate indicated on the container. It is useful to mix the fertilizer with coarse sand at planting time.

FORKING OVER THE GROUND
Concentrated fertilizers should be worked into the planting site with a fork to ensure they are incorporated into the soil.

PLANTING DEPTHS

Once the site has been well prepared, the pleasure of planting can begin. Most bulbs need to be planted at about three to five times their own depth in the ground. There are exceptions, however: tulips can be planted even deeper, while rhizomes of the wood anemone need to be placed just below the surface of the soil in well-rotted compost. If you find that a plant fails to flower, experiment by planting the bulb more deeply; this sometimes stops the bulb from splitting into smaller offsets and may induce flowering.

In light, sandy soils it is best to plant more deeply but, whatever the soil, space the bulbs about two to three bulb-widths apart, then firm the site and water in. Some bulbs, like bluebells, have specially adapted, strong roots to help the bulbs find their own level.

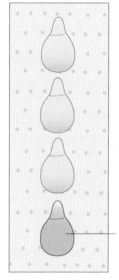

BULB DEPTHS
Although a depth of 2–3 times their own height is sufficient for some bulbs, others need to be planted deeper, at 4 to 5 times their height. Bulbs flower more regularly if planted at greater depths where they are less affected by climatic changes.

Bulb planted at four times its depth

PREPARATION FOR NATURALIZING BULBS

Autumn is the best time for planting most bulbs in naturalized situations. Wait for damp conditions when the disturbed grass will soon grow back and the ground will be easier to cultivate. If groups of small bulbs like crocuses or fritillaries are to be planted, use a spade to cut an H-shape in the grass, cut under the grass, and fold it back to reveal the soil. The soil can be loosened, fertilized, and the bulbs planted. The grass flaps are then folded back and the area well watered. If larger bulbs are to be planted, then a bulb-planting tool, which can take out a plug of soil 6in (15cm) deep, is best used. A little fertilizer should be added to the soil before the bulb is planted.

1 To plan the display but still retain a natural look, randomly scatter colored blocks to represent the colors of the flowers.

2 Then use a bulb planter to make holes in the places indicated by the colored blocks. A hand-sized version of this tool is available.

PLANTING BULBS

BULBS ARE QUICK TO GIVE A COLORFUL DISPLAY wherever they are planted. This near-instant effect gives the new gardener encouragement and the experienced gardener a chance to move bulbs regularly, without any detrimental effect. Some bulbs are among the few plants that are actually improved by being moved, split up, and replanted annually. Container bulbs can be planted straight out into the border as soon as the flowers have finished in late spring.

PLANTING "IN THE GREEN"

Bulbs that are prone to desiccation, such as snowdrops, snowflakes, and aconites, are best planted just after flowering with the leaves intact, called "in the green." Plant these bulbs in soil that has been loosened and fertilized, making sure that they never dry out. To avoid any chance of infection, dust any wounded surfaces of the bulbs with a fungicide powder, such as powdered sulfur, before planting. Be careful to plant the bulbs back at their original depth. There is a papery sheath around the bulb that should be present when planting.

IN THE GREEN
The new planting depth should match the old. Aim for the point where the leaf meets the papery sheath at the top of the bulb. Spread out the roots, and always water the site well.

PLANTING IN THE OPEN

Try to find a site that is suitable for the bulbs you are planting. Most will need full exposure to the sun, but a few, such as camassias, prefer a shady site. Dig the site, remove any roots, and fork over the base to aerate the soil deeply. Add a dry fertilizer and place your bulbs in a hole of the correct depth. To achieve a random pattern, dig an irregularly shaped hole. If large single bulbs are being planted, then a bulb planter makes the job easier, but a slim spade or trowel will suffice.

1 **Fork over the area,** then dig the hole to the depth required. Add the dry fertilizer (*see inset*), and place the bulbs in the hole.

2 **Arrange the bulbs at random,** making sure that they remain upright as you replace the soil. Cover the bulbs and firm gently, then label the area.

PLANTING IN A CONTAINER

Most bulbs are suitable for growing in a container as long as the pot is large enough for the chosen bulb and the drainage is adequate, or the roots may rot. As soon as the flowers are over, the pots can be placed out of sight. Always give the bulbs as much depth for root growth as possible. This reduces the watering needs. Try to use a soil-based potting mix, which will retain moisture and nutrients for longer than a soilless one. Plant the bulbs as deeply as in the garden and cover the surface with a ⅛–¼in (4–5mm) layer of grit. This prevents soil splash and reduces evaporation.

Bulbs should point upward. This is not easy to tell with tubers such as corydalis.

1 **Lay a piece of screening** over the hole before adding soil mix. Place the bulbs on top of the mix, growing points upward.

2 **Top dress with grit,** and water well to settle the soil mix. Insert a label to identify the bulbs. Keep the soil moist.

BURYING A CONTAINER IN A BORDER

This is an excellent method of discreetly filling gaps or of seasonally noting the changes within a border. The container can be a simple plastic pot or a lattice basket more usually used for pond plantings. The lattice baskets must be buried at all times, because the roots will be active beyond the confines of the basket, and so a resting place in the garden is needed for when the containers are not in season. The area around the sunken pots needs aerating with soil and compost so that any lifting and replanting does as little damage to the roots as possible. These baskets are also very useful for keeping track of your bulbs.

Check the bulbs are upright

1 **Plant the bulbs** at the usual depth in a soil mix to suit them and a bulb's width apart to allow for growth. The basket can be left in for a year or so to mature.

2 **Bury the basket** just below the surface of the ground, attach a label to the basket, and water in. A bark mulch is an attractive and easily removed topdressing.

ROUTINE CARE

ONCE BULBS ARE PLANTED, they provide years of pleasure, requiring little aftercare. In summer, when the foliage has died down, it is best to remove the leaves and rake over the resulting holes in the ground to stop insects having access to the bulbs. After a few years, even if the bulbs are doing well, any dense clumps may need thinning out. Lift during the resting season, separate out, and replant. Tender bulbs, such as gladioli, need lifting before the onset of winter.

SUPPORTING

It would be marvelous if all bulbous plants could be freestanding, without artificial aid. Unfortunately, this is not the case, and a few do need extra support. Vulnerable plants that may need staking are lilies, gladioli, dahlias, and some camassias. In pots, hyacinths and narcissi will need a little light tying. There are many commercial supports available – hoops, half-circles, Y-stakes, and grids of various types – and these are mostly discreet and reusable. However, many gardeners still rely on the traditional stake-and-twine method to hold the stem or stems. Soft, green jute is still the most unobtrusive twine for this work. Whatever you plan, start early, getting the structure in place before the wind damages the plant. In an emergency the half-circle and Y-stakes can be eased into position to support the stems that have begun to lean.

▲ STAKING A GLADIOLUS
Insert the stake next to the stem when 6in (15cm) tall and tie with soft garden twine in a figure-eight loop. When the plant is at bud stage, tie again just below the bud.

◄ STAKING A GROUP OF LILIES
Some lilies can be supported by carefully pushing in stakes among the bulbs and tying in each stem with a figure-eight loop. When mature, the lilies will help support each other.

Fertilizing after Flowering

When the flowers begin to fade, the leaves will continue to work at building up the strength of the bulb.

To aid this process, a regular liquid fertilizer that is high in potash (such as tomato fertilizer) is very beneficial. This feeding will have the effect of prolonging the above-ground life of the plant and will build up larger bulbs with the potential to flower and form offsets. Watering with a liquid fertilizer can also rectify any trace element deficiency in the soil, such as a lack of magnesium, which can lead to premature yellowing of the leaves. Once the leaves begin to decay, cease watering, because the bulbs will need a dry period in the summer.

LIQUID FERTILIZING
Apply to both the foliage and the soil for maximum uptake. Consider diluting to half the recommended strength.

Mulching

During the resting period, mulch bulb areas with well-rotted organic material, such as mushroom soil or compost. In the rock garden or raised bed, a finer mulch (graded by sieving) should be mixed with balanced fertilizer then topdressed with gravel.

APPLYING MULCH
Organic material is best applied when bulbs are resting but can be added at other times as long as the soil is moist.

Using Inorganic Fertilizer

Commercially available preparations, such as tomato fertilizer or pelleted fertilizer, enable the gardener to add precisely the desired amount of fertilizer to the plant at the required intervals. Always read the instructions carefully and use the fertilizer regularly at greater dilution rather than in one large dose. If the soil is dry, moisten it first; otherwise, the fertilizer may run off the soil and away from the plant. Never apply directly onto foliage in direct sunlight, because this might damage the leaves. In free-draining sandy soils, much of the nutrient content of the fertilizer may be washed away very quickly by heavy rain.

TYPES OF INORGANIC FERTILIZERS

- Tomato fertilizer is high in potassium and is ideal for promoting flower production.
- Granular fertilizers have an even spread of nitrogen, phosphorus, and potassium for general fertilizing.
- Specialized fertilizers come in combinations of nitrogen, phosphorus, and potassium in ratios to suit all plants. The ratio of 1:2:2 is ideal for bulbs. Many mixes contain trace elements essential for healthy growth.

TOMATO FERTILIZER

REMOVING LEAVES AND LIFTING

RESIST THE TEMPTATION to remove the foliage soon after the flowers have faded, because this will weaken the bulb and reduce the flowering next season. Wait until the foliage is just turning yellow before you remove it. The leaves die down at differing rates, with corydalis and snowdrops ready for clearing by late spring, whereas colchicum leaves must wait until early summer. You can lift bulbs while dormant or can move them while still in leaf.

REMOVING FOLIAGE

While the leaves are yellow, some will still cling to the bulb, so if you pull them off, you risk bringing the dormant bulb to the surface. It is, therefore, better to cut off the foliage. Some summer-flowering bulbs, such as alliums and camassias, have leaves that are already dying down at flowering time. If they are not hidden by other foliage, you can cut them off without detriment to the bulb.

CUTTING BACK TO THE GROUND
Naturalized bulb foliage is best cut off to ground level using shears. This removes the surrounding grass and neatens the site.

LIFTING BULBS

After a few years, the flowering display of a group of bulbs may begin to wane, indicating that it is time to lift and thin the bulbs. While the bulbs are dormant, insert a fork some distance back from the clump, then lift. The bulbs will probably be very congested and of many sizes.

Most gardeners simply replant the largest and healthiest bulbs in a fresh part of the garden. If large numbers are wanted, the smaller bulbs and the offsets from the larger ones can be grown on in a nursery patch. After a few seasons they will start to flower and can be moved.

MOVING BULBS "IN THE GREEN"

You may need to move plants during the "wrong" season, while they are still green. Treat them like other plants: dig up the root ball intact and replant immediately. Water well. You could pot the bulb and keep it in a shady place until the leaves die down naturally.

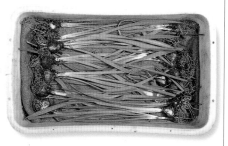

MOVING "IN THE GREEN"
Galanthus and Leucojum are ideally moved while still in leaf, but this treatment can be used for many other kinds of bulb.

STORING BULBS

BULBS USED IN CONTAINERS or in any form of seasonal bedding may need to be stored safely until they are replanted in the next season. If you need to clear part of the garden by moving bulbs while the leaves are still green, be careful to lift the root ball intact and replant in a pot or shady part of the garden. Label the spot and keep it watered until the leaves begin to decay. Once the leaves have turned yellow, the bulbs can then be lifted and prepared for storage.

STORAGE CONDITIONS

Most bulbs, like tulips, crocuses, and daffodils, can be stored. Dry bulbs are best stored in a paper bag or cardboard box, labeled, and kept in a cool, airy place. Check them every few weeks and remove any bulbs that show signs of rotting.

There are a few bulbs, however, such as erythroniums and wood anemones, that need cool, moist conditions to remain in good health. These bulbs can be lifted in the same way but need setting in a pot of rich soil mix or a reserve bed and should be labeled ready for careful lifting when required. Alternatively, these bulbs can be mixed with a little vermiculite, placed in a clean plastic bag, and stored at 43°F (6°C). A salad container in a refrigerator is ideal for this procedure.

1 **Clean off any soil** by hand or with a dry paintbrush and remove the old foliage and any old dried roots. Keep only the healthy, unblemished bulbs.

2 **Make sure** that the bulbs are clean and dry before dusting them with a fungicide. Shake off any excess, place in a clean paper bag, and label. Keep them cool and dry.

WINTER STORAGE
Most bulbs, such as daffodils, can be stored in dry, cool conditions until needed. Use a cardboard or wooden box kept in dark, dry place.

STORING BULBS

• Select only the best bulbs.
• Corms such as gladioli should be placed in a box to dry out prior to cleaning and storage.
• Dip dry corms and tubers in fungicide to avoid rot.
• To store gladiolus corms, snap the old corms from the new, discarding the old corms and keeping the new corms dry and frost free until replanted.
• Check regularly for disease.

FORCING PREPARED BULBS

ALONG-ESTABLISHED PRACTICE is to plant specially prepared bulbs in containers and keep them cold and dark to induce them to flower early, providing color and cheer during the winter months. Hyacinths and some daffodils are favorites for this treatment. They are best moved to a cool room or conservatory once the leaves begin to show and brought into the living room only for the period of flowering, when the flowers and scent can be enjoyed.

HYACINTHS

Prepared hyacinths should be bought as soon as they appear in the garden center or nursery and planted in bulb fiber or soil mix, close together, with the tips of the bulbs just showing above the mix. Water so that the mix is damp, but not soggy. Place in a cold frame, the refrigerator, or inside a black plastic bag kept in the garage, and continue to keep them just moist. After about eight weeks, buds will be visible and it will be time to bring the pot into a light, but not sunny, position to flower. A cool room or conservatory is ideal. Stake the plants if necessary.

SEASONAL FAVORITES

As long as the selection is marked as a "prepared" bulb you can be sure of very early (midwinter) flowering.

Hyacinths include 'Anna Marie', a soft pink, 'L'Innocence', which is compact and white, and 'Ostara', a deep blue. There are also multiple-stemmed hyacinths with a similar color range available.

Daffodils such as 'Paper White' and 'Grand Soleil d'Or' should be started in bright but not strong light. They are best grown in cool rooms so they do not become lanky and need staking.

A 6in (15cm) pot will accommodate 3 hyacinth bulbs

At this stage of growth, the pot can be brought into a cool, light room

1 Choose an attractive container and plant three or five bulbs in moist bulb fiber or soil mix, with their tips just visible. Place in a cool, dark place.

2 When the flower buds are visible, albeit rather yellow, bring them into a cool but bright position to grow quickly and flower. They will soon turn green in the light.

GROWING HYACINTHS IN WATER

This method is ideal for children, because plant growth can be seen easily. A glass lor plastic container should be filled to the neck with water to which a few pieces of charcoal are added, in order to keep the water clear and sweet smelling. Always use prepared hyacinth bulbs and set them in a cool, dark place, as for soil-planted bulbs. Once the bulb has strong root growth, it can then be placed on a bright, but not sunny, windowsill to flower. The only care needed is to fill up of the water level. Once the bulb has flowered, it is best discarded.

1 Rest the bulb just above the water level, being careful to leave a small gap.

Leave the vase for some 8 weeks or so in the dark

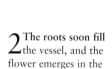

CARE IN WATER

• Keep the water filled up to just beneath the basal plate.
• If the water starts to smell, replace it with fresh water as you would for cut flowers.
• Regularly turn the container to keep the flower stem upright and stable.
• Although the bulb could be grown on, it has been without nutrients and is best discarded once the flower is finished. If you want to plant it out, do so carefully, spreading the roots, and water in.

2 The roots soon fill the vessel, and the flower emerges in the usual way.

A perfect set of roots necessary to support the emerging flower spike

FORCING AMARYLLIS

The large-flowered amaryllis (*Hippeastrum*) are very versatile plants, and it is now possible to buy and flower them at almost any time of the year. Colors range from pure white to pink to strong red. All of them, including the smaller-flowered varieties, are equally easy to grow and flower. Unlike many other forced bulbs, these need warm and light conditions from the beginning to flower and grow well. When grown near a window, they do require turning to straighten the flowering stem. Keep the plant cool (50°F/10°C) and dry through the autumn until midwinter, when the leaves can be removed and the top of the old soil mix replaced with new. Bring into warmth and start regular watering and fertilizing. These bulbs should be repotted only when the roots tightly fill the pot. You can buy amaryllis in autumn as boxed kits.

COMMERCIALLY AVAILABLE KITS
Plant the large bulbs with only the bottom half covered by the soil mix. Water sparingly until the leaves and roots a have begun to grow, then water freely.

Kits include soil mix, cultural instructions, and a pot as well as the bulb

GROWING YOUR OWN BULBS

MOST BULBS NATURALLY MULTIPLY to survive. To obtain more plants, the gardener simply needs to tap into this process at the appropriate time. Bulbs can be teased apart, but tubers, such as aconites, need to be cut into smaller pieces if more plants are required. During dormancy is usually the best time to propagate bulbs, and this is most easily achieved by lifting the whole clump, gently it teasing apart, and replanting the healthiest bulbs.

STARTING BULBS FROM SEED

This is another simple but often slow method of propagation. Gather the seeds in paper bags, so that any excess moisture is absorbed by the paper and does not lead to the seeds rotting. Bulb seeds are usually quite large and easily handled, but they do need cleaning before being sown. Gently winnow to remove the chaff and infertile seeds. Then sow in a prepared pot or store the seeds in a dry, airy, shaded spot, such as a shed, until sowing time. This is generally in early autumn for germination the following spring, although it may take two years.

▶ GATHERING A RIPE SEEDHEAD
Take the bag to the seedhead, so seeds are not lost as the head is snapped from the stem. Shake the head to release the seeds.

1 **Choose a pot** to suit the number of seeds being sown. A 3in (7cm) pot will be adequate for a fair number of seeds: do not sow them too closely, or the potential growth will be inhibited.

2 **Cover the seeds** with ¼in (5mm) of sieved seed soil mix. Do not press down, but just tap the pot to settle the mix. Very large seeds will need a greater depth of mix to cover them.

3 **Cover the soil mix** evenly with ¼in (5mm) of grit, so that the mix is hidden. This will deter the growth of liverwort and mosses and also protect the seeds from being dislodged during watering.

DIVIDING FLESHY-ROOTED BULBS

Some larger bulbs, such as lilies and nerines, have very thick, fleshy roots that although produced annually, persist as useless husks from year to year. Eventually, the soil needs refreshing around the bulbs and the old roots teasing out. When the bulbs are dying down, take a fork and carefully insert it some distance from the clump, then gently lift. You may find some active white roots among the old; try to keep these intact while you discard the old roots, leaves, and any damaged or diseased bulbs. From the remaining bulbs, plant only the best in enriched soil, and water well. Cut dahlia tubers in half in spring, making sure each half has a growing point, and plant out.

1 Divide a large area into manageable clumps. Push the fork under the bulbs from one side, then repeat from another side if there is resistance. Lever the clump free of the soil.

2 Separate out the bulbs, once lifted, carefully pulling them apart by hand, if possible. Discard the old roots and leaves, but keep any young roots.

EASILY PROPAGATED BULBS

Some bulbs can be divided when resting. Offsets are attached to the sides of the parent bulb and can be eased apart and planted in their own space.
Galanthus (snowdrop)
Narcissus (daffodil)
Scilla

Some bulbs seed profusely: lift young bulbs as you see them. If you want more, gather ripe seedheads and sow them in a pot (see the opposite page for more information).
Allium
Cyclamen
Eranthis

3 Clean the bulbs gently, then select the very best bulbs for replanting in a newly prepared site. If the old site is to be reused, work in some bone meal or similar fertilizer as well as some new soil before planting.

AVOIDING PROBLEMS

BULBS ARE NO MORE PRONE TO PROBLEMS than other plants. Always buy healthy, fresh stock for planting, and if you are given a suspect-looking bulb, harden your heart and dispose of it. Always dispose of any diseased bulbs by burning or placing in a sealed bag in the trash, never on the compost pile. Once you have healthy bulbs, good gardening habits will prevent many of the possible problems from occurring and reduce the need for any chemical or biological controls.

IDENTIFYING PROBLEMS

Any problem with a bulb results in poor or stunted growth. As soon as you see abnormal growth, lift the bulb with the surrounding soil and examine it carefully. It may be that the damage is physical, such as from a slug, or cultural. If the roots are short or nonexistent, the drainage may need improving. Dig deeply and replant, watering the bulbs well. Occasionally, a stem may grow grotesquely as if many stems are fused together. This is fasciation and is not contagious. It is often the result of some damage in early growth.

BULB BLINDNESS

Occasionally, bulbs form buds that fail to flower. This is often a result of overcrowding and a lack of nutrients; it is rarely a disease. Bulb blindness is usually remedied by lifting and replanting in fertilized soil.

BASAL ROT
This fungal disease has no cure. Safe disposal (not on the compost pile) to stop its spread to healthy bulbs is the only recourse.

A brown stain spreads around the scales of the bulb

DEALING WITH PESTS

• Be vigilant and remove any pests by hand.
• Keep a neat garden so that there are fewer places for pests to live and breed.
• Use pesticide sparingly, as a last resort, avoiding contact with any other wildlife.
• In greenhouses, try simple traps, such as sticky papers, and other nonbiological means of keeping pests in check.
• The introduction of predatory and parasitic insects to greenhouses can be an effective method of controlling specific pests (e.g. whitefly by a parasitic wasp).
• Encourage birds by setting up nestboxes. Some birds feed hundreds of insects a day to its young.

BULB FLIES

A number of insects use bulbs as a host in their lifecycles. The narcissus bulb fly looks like a small bumblebee and lays its eggs on the neck of the bulb in early summer. Mound soil over the holes left by the old stem and leaves as they die down. There may be remaining eggs or insects in the soil, so do not replant bulbs in the same area for several years or they may also be affected.

STORAGE ROT

Infections can enter bulbs and tubers such as dahlias while they are in storage. Discard any rotting material before the disease has time to spread to other tubers and bulbs. If dry bulbs develop gray velvety mold (*botrytis*), they must be destroyed and adjacent bulbs dusted with fungicide.

A CALENDAR OF SEASONAL REMINDERS

SUMMER

• As the leaves of early-flowering bulbs die down, lift and divide any that are overcrowded.

• Gather dry seed in paper bags and store in a cool dry place. Remember to label the bags.

• Clear away dying foliage to neaten the border and avoid the spread of disease.

• Rake over holes left in the soil by old bulb stems to lessen the chance of insects such as the narcissus bulb fly laying eggs in the tunnel, giving the larvae easy access to the bulb. Finally, lightly mulch the entire area.

• Plant out pot-grown summer- and autumn-flowering bulbs to fill gaps in the border or to enhance a color scheme.

• Repot winter and spring bulbs, now they are resting. Some may require completely repotting with new soil mix; others just need an inspection and topping up with fresh mix with some extra general-purpose fertilizer.

• Tie gladiolus and tall dahlias to stakes for support.

• Buy new bulbs from your local garden center or order from bulb catalogs.

AUTUMN

• Plant commercial bulbs as quickly as possible. Daffodils can begin root growth as early as late summer, if the conditions are right.

• Prepare heavy or compacted soil for planting by digging deeply, adding grit to aid aeration. Sprinkle a general-purpose fertilizer into the planting hole, and plant the bulbs at two to five times their own depth (or deeper, depending on the bulb; *see p.51*).

• Lift dahlias and gladiolus and prepare for winter storage.

ADDING FERTILIZER

• Mark the location of your bulbs, with labels or by drawing a plan, to avoid disturbance later.

• Make sure that there is sufficient space in the borders for autumn bulbs by neatening any summer foliage so that the flowers can be fully enjoyed.

• In early autumn, plant containers with specially prepared bulbs to flower in midwinter.

WINTER

• Clear away any old foliage that might impede fresh growth, and mulch the site.

• Add a general-purpose fertilizer to the surrounding soil.

STORING BULBS OVER WINTER

• Store bulbs in a box in a cool, frost free place and check regularly for disease.

• It is possible to move groups of bulbs at this time of year if the soil is not frozen. Dig up the clump and place in the new position. Water in to settle the roots.

• Sow commercial bulb seed as soon as received and cover the soil mix with ¼in (5mm) grit to restrict evaporation and deter the growth of liverwort and moss. Expose the pots to the weather in a shady position.

• If leaves on indoor plants show signs of disease such as mosaic virus streaking, dispose of the entire plant.

• Bring forced bulbs into a cool place to flower.

• Order bulb catalogs and begin planning.

SPRING

• Replant pot-grown bulbs bought for an instant effect, and water in.

• Snowdrops and snowflakes bought "in the green" should be planted without delay and copiously watered in.

• Check for any gray mold (*Botrytis*), especially prevalent if the season is dry, and consider spraying with a fungicide to reduce infection.

• In windy sites, stake tall bulbs, such as crown imperials and lilies, before they are damaged.

• In late spring, plant out tender bulbs such as gladioli and begonias.

• Regular deadheading concentrates energy into bulb development rather than seed production.

• In late spring, clear away the yellowing bulb foliage to neaten the border and to eliminate the homes for slugs and snails.

• Container bulbs grown for winter display can be stored in a cool out of the way place, until time for repotting in summer.

• Fertilize potted bulbs with liquid fertilizer.

CHOICE BULBS FOR THE GARDEN

THE FOLLOWING LIST is a representative selection from the wide range of adaptable and easily grown bulbs for sale in nurseries and garden centers. Traditionally available in late summer and early autumn as dry bulbs, they may be offered in pots as flowering plants, enabling you to see their exact color and height. The choice of bulbs is rich and diverse, so one that is not listed here is not necessarily inferior to another that is featured.

▨ *Prefers full sun* ▨ *Prefers partial shade* ◊ *Prefers well-drained soil* ◉ *Prefers moist soil* **Small** *Up to 12in (30cm)* **Medium** *12–36in (30–90cm)* **Tall** *Over 36in (90cm)* *Hardiness zone ranges are given as Zx-x* ◕ *Indicates a frost-tender plant that may be grown indoors*

A

Allium

In the huge genus of onions, these of ornamental value have impressive flowerheads and strappy, pungent leaves. All of these species flower in summer and multiply quickly by seed, forming colonies.
A. cernuum (nodding onion) is a small to medium grower with nodding flowers varying from white to rose-purple. 'Hidcote' is taller and plum-purple. ▨◊Z4-10
A. cristophii is a medium onion with a 6in (15cm) flowerhead of metallic pink-purple flowers. ▨◊Z5-8
A. hollandicum, syn.
A. aflatunense of gardens, is a tall onion, with a 4in (10cm) pink-purple head. ▨◊Z4-10

ALLIUM MOLY

The flowerheads of both *A. cristophii* and the smaller *A. hollandicum* are excellent as dried-flower decorations. *A. moly* (golden garlic) is a small plant with bright yellow flowers in a 2in (5cm) flowerhead. ▨◊Z3-9

A. cristophii p.9
A. insubricum p.37
A. oreophilum p.37

Amaryllis

This is a genus of just one exotic-looking species that flowers in the early autumn. *A. belladonna* is a bulbous plant of medium height originating in South Africa, with thick, green to purple stems and around six large, trumpet-shaped pink flowers, each up to 4in (10cm) long, that are produced in the autumn. The flowers are followed by long, strap-shaped leaves. Plant on the sunny side of a wall to give some winter protection where marginally hardy. Where not hardy, amaryllis are best grown in a cool greenhouse. ▨◊Z7-10

◀ LILY-FLOWERED *KAUFMANNIANA* GROUP TULIPS *A beautiful yellow hybrid of medium height.*

ANEMONE CORONARIA
'LORD LIEUTENANT'

Anemone (Windflower)
This genus grows in varied habitats from cool woods to rocky mountains.
A. blanda is a small, tuberous plant with daisylike flowers, up to 1½in (4cm) in diameter, in colors that vary from blue through purple to pink and white, often with a pale eye. It likes sun or partial shade and spreads quickly by seed. ▨–▨◊Z4-8
A. coronaria is a small to medium, tuberous plant with showy flowers good for cutting that can be red, blue, or white, in spring.
The De Caen Group and the St. Brigid Group are collective names for (respectively) single-flowered and double-flowered selections of this species, in a wide color range. ▨◊Z8-10
A. nemorosa is a small, rhizomatous woodland anemone with many cultivars in white and shades of blue that brighten early spring. It has attractive, mid-green dissected foliage once the flowers have finished. ▨◊Z4-8

A. blanda p.8
A. pavonina p.9
Also recommended:
A. × fulgens

B

Begonia
Tuberous bedding begonias are essentially summer-flowering, mostly double-flowered hybrids, many with showy flowers, in a wide range of colors. They are small to medium in height. The tubers should be lifted in the autumn before the first frost and stored frost-free until they are replanted in spring. ▨◊❂
Multiflora Begonias p.20

C

Camassia (Quamash)
These bulbs flower in late spring to early summer. Their restrained shades and ease of cultivation contribute to their gaining popularity. They will thrive in any ordinary border and do not require a dry summer rest. *C. cusickii* is a

CAMASSIA LEICHTLINII

CANNA 'ASSAULT'

medium, meadowland bulb from North America. It has a few channeled leaves and tall spires of pale to deep blue, starry flowers. ▨◊Z3-10
C. leichtlinii is taller, with creamy white flowers. There is a double form 'Semiplena' in cultivation. ▨◊Z4-10
C. quamash p.25

Canna
These tall, rhizomatous plants have paddle-shaped leaves – themselves very architectural – topped with brightly colored, three-petaled flowers in summer. Where not reliably hardy they must be lifted in autumn, stored in a frost-free environment (*see p.57*), and replanted in spring.
'Assault' (*p.31*) has scarlet and orange flowers and purple-brown leaves. 'King Midas' has dark leaves and golden yellow flowers. ▨◊Z8-11
Also recommended:
Tropicanna

Cardiocrinum (Giant lily)
This genus of three species is from Southeast Asia. All are

large plants that require rich soil, with moisture during the summer. These bulbs have perennial roots that must not be allowed to dry out. They take several years to reach maturity and flower, after which they die, usually leaving several offsets.

C. giganteum is a lilylike bulb with attractive, heart-shaped leaves, a tall stem, and scented, trumpet-shaped flowers in summer.
▣◊Z7-9

Chionodoxa

(Glory of the snow)
This genus from West Turkey, Crete, and Cyprus is related to *Scilla* (*p.76*). These small bulbous plants are easy to grow in sun or partial shade. They seed profusely and flower quickly from seed.
C. luciliae has up to 12 small, starry, blue flowers per stem. A pink-flowered form is also available. ▣–▣◊Z3-9

Colchicum

These corms are sometimes referred to as "autumn crocuses." To add to the confusion, there are many autumn-flowering crocuses.
C. byzantinum is a small, prolific plant with soft lilac, starry flowers, 4in (10cm) in diameter, in the autumn. These are followed in spring by large, ribbed leaves. There is also a white form.
C. speciosum 'Album', also small, has white, goblet-shaped flowers on lime green stems in autumn. They stand well for days and are very weather-resistant.
C. 'Waterlily' is small and vigorous, with up to five fully double, pinkish flowers per corm. Even when they fall over the flowers remain attractive. These large-flowered selections look good on the sunny side of shrubs or among herbaceous plants, which will disguise their dying leaves in summer.
▣◊Z4-9
C. 'Waterlily' *p.38*
Also recommended:
C. tenorei

Corydalis syn. Pseudofumaria

The tuberous corydalis is widespread in the Northern Hemisphere. The following are easy to grow, with early, frost-resistant flowers.
C. malkensis, syn. *C. caucasica* var. *alba*, is a small plant with creamy, tubular flowers in early spring. It is happy in sun or partial shade and excellent for colonizing beds by seed. In early spring, it blankets the ground in white, withering quickly in the late spring sun.
C. solida, syn. *C. halleri*, has flowers that vary from pink to red and purple, with some white examples. Very easily grown, this small plant is best in full sun, where it remains compact and vibrant.
▣–▣◊Z5-7

Crinum

Widespread in the Southern Hemisphere, crinums include one frost-hardy species.
C. × *powellii* is a tall South African hybrid and will grow happily in a well-drained, sheltered site. The long leaves are followed by tall stems topped with pink, fragrant, flared trumpets that are 4in (10cm) long. 'Album' is white.
▣◊Z7-10

CARDIOCRINUM GIGANTEUM

COLCHICUM SPECIOSUM 'ALBUM'

CRINUM × POWELLII

CROCUSES

All crocuses are small and can be chosen to provide color in the open garden from autumn through spring. ◊▩ Zones vary

Spring-flowering
Crocus ancyrensis has orange, rounded flowers. It is suited to a sunny bed or container. Z 5 - 8
C. chrysanthus 'Blue Pearl' has white flowers that are overlaid with lilac-blue and have yellow throats.
C. chrysanthus 'Cream Beauty' has a small, cream flower with a deep yellow throat. *C. chrysanthus* 'Ladykiller' has flowers with a white background and a purple mark on the outside. All *chrysanthus* are Z 3 - 8
C. 'Dutch Yellow' is a vigorous crocus with orange-yellow flowers good for naturalizing. Z 3 - 8
C. sieberi 'Albus' (syn. 'Bowles White') is white with a yellow throat. Z 3 - 8

CROCUS TOMMASINIANUS
'RUBY GIANT'

C. sieberi 'Hubert Edelsten' is a pale lilac flower, with the three shining purple outer petals marked with a white line. Z 3 - 8
C. tommasinianus (Z 3 - 8) is a consummate survivor and spreader. There is a white form, f. *albus*.
C. tommasinianus 'Ruby Giant' is sterile and good for light soil, where seeding crocuses can be invasive.

Autumn-flowering
C. speciosus 'Oxonian' (Z 3 - 8) is a dark violet crocus up to 4in (10cm) tall. The thin leaves appear in late winter. A good crocus for naturalizing in grass or around shrubs in light shade.
C. medius has bright purple flowers. It does well in sun or dappled shade. Z 3 - 8
C. ochroleucus produces its creamy white flowers in late autumn. Z 5 - 8

CROCUS SIEBERI
'HUBERT EDELSTEN'

CROCOSMIA
'STAR OF THE EAST'

Crocosmia (Montbretia)
This plant is easy to grow and forms self-supporting clumps. It is a medium-height plant, superb in sun or partial shade as long as the soil is well drained but moist. Those grown are usually hybrids of the South African species.
C. × crocosmiiflora 'Dusky Maiden' has unusual, deep bronze, lance-shaped leaves with funnel-shaped, brown-orange flowers in late summer.
C. × crocosmiiflora 'Star of the East' is of medium height with starry, orange flowers, nearly 4in (10cm) across in late summer to early autumn.
C. 'Lucifer' is tall and robust, with bright red flowers in midsummer.
▨ – ▩ ◊ Z 6 - 9
C. × crocosmiiflora
  'Gerbe d'Or' *p.46*
  'Jackanapes' *p.47*
Also recommended:
C. × crocosmiiflora 'Emily McKenzie'

Cyclamen
A beautiful group of tuberous plants. Many are scented, and most are easily cultivated.

C. coum is a small, late-winter flowering cyclamen. The round leaves can range from plain green to silver or pewter, with many combination in between, while the flowers range from white to carmine-red. These cyclamen are very effective when planted around deciduous shrubs, providing color at the most drab time of year. ⬛◊Z 5 - 9
C. hederifolium (syn.
C. neopolitanum) is larger than *C. coum*, with triangular leaves and flowers produced in early autumn. They seed around very attractively once established and look best planted in groups, rather than scattered. There is also an entirely silver-leaved selection that seems to produce mostly silver-marked seedlings. ⬛◊Z 8 - 9
C. persicum cultivars are sold as houseplants at every florist and plant center. The flowers range from white to carmine and vary greatly in shape. Once the flowers and leaves begin to wither, the plant should be rested away from sunlight and kept fairly dry. ⬛◊✿
C. cilicum p.39
C. coum p.11
C. hederifolium p.7
Also recommended:
C. repandum

Cyrtanthus (Fire lily)
A genus of tender bulbs from South Africa. The following species requires a drier rest in winter before growth and watering start in spring.
C. elatus (Scarborough lily) is a medium bulb that, in cold climates, makes an easy-to-grow and attractive addition to the windowsill.

This plant has strap-shaped leaves and scarlet, funnel-shaped flowers on thick stems in summer. ⬛◊✿

D

Dahlia
Tuberous-rooted plants from Central and South America, dahlias can be simply grouped into the tall border varieties and the shorter bedding types. There are thousands of cultivars of this plant with flowers in numerous colors, heights, and shapes. Dahlias flower from midsummer until the frosts of autumn, when the tubers should be lifted and stored frost-free *(see p.57)* and then replanted in the spring. Dahlias are hugely popular, and the following is just a small selection of what is available. 'Bishop of Llandaff' is a medium to tall, semi-double dahlia with red petals and stunningly dark foliage. 'Charlie Two' is a tall plant with medium-sized flowers. It has bright yellow, multi-petaled flowerheads.

DAHLIA 'FASCINATION'

'Fascination' is a small, peony-flowered bedding plant with dark pink flowers and dark bronze foliage.
'Glorie van Heemstede' is a bright yellow waterlily dahlia of medium height.
'Grenidor Pastelle' is a plant of medium height and has a salmon-pink flower with a cream center.
'Mi Wong' is a medium pompon dahlia with flowers that are strong pink in color. ⬛◊Z 8 - 1 1
Unwins Dwarf Group p.46
Also recommended:
'Arabian Night'

E

Eranthis (Winter aconite)
A tuberous plant, best in cool, semi-shaded positions.
E. hyemalis has yellow, cup-shaped flowers in spring. It is small, but it will spread quickly by seed. Winter aconites are easy to incorporate in any garden since, by mid-spring, the foliage can be cleared away. ⬛◊Z 4 - 9

ERANTHIS HYEMALIS

EUCOMIS BICOLOR

Erythronium
(Dog's-tooth violet,
Trout lily)
Bulbous plants with two
basal leaves, mostly from
North America, with a few
from Europe and Asia.
Erythroniums should be
bought as pot plants or as
slightly damp bulbs, since
they resent being dry.
E. dens-canis is a small,
spring-flowering plant with
mid-green leaves marbled
purple-brown. The flowers,
which are white, pink, or
lilac, are pendent and arch
gracefully backward. Z 3 - 9
E. 'Pagoda' is a vigorous
plant, with bronze-marked
leaves and between two and
five yellow flowers, each
with a brown central ring.
'Pagoda' may grow to
medium height. Z 4 - 9
E. revolutum (American trout
lily) is a small but very
beautiful plant, with bright
green leaves and mottled
brown and pink, backward
arching flowers. This species
will form colonies. Z 5 - 9
🄰◊
Also recommended:
E. californicum

Eucomis (Pineapple flower, Pineapple lily)
These bulbs from South
Africa have strong roots
requiring lots of moisture.
A medium, late-summer
flowering bulb, *Eucomis
bicolor* benefits from a mulch
in winter where marginally
hardy. The tall flower spikes
have green flowers, each
margined in purple, with a
pineapple-like tuft of leaves
at the top.
🄰◊ Z 8 - 10
E. bicolor p.10
E. pole-evansii p.39

F

Fritillaria (Fritillary)
All plants in this genus have
pendent, bell-shaped flowers.
F. imperialis (Crown imperial,
Z 5 - 9) is a medium spring
bulb with whorls of leaves
and stately flower spikes, each
with up to eight hanging, bell-
shaped flowers in yellow,
orange, or red. Each flower
stalk is topped with a tuft of
leaves. *F. meleagris* (Snake's
head fritillary, Z 3 - 8), is a

FRITILLARIA MELEAGRIS

European species and is
very tolerant of many garden
situations – from a sunny
border to naturalization in
short grass. It is short-
stemmed, with thin, grayish
leaves, and has checkered,
nodding, bell-shaped, purplish
and sometimes white flowers.
F. persica 'Adiyaman', Z 6 - 8,
is a tall plant with a spire of
up to 30 small purple bells in
early spring above a tuft of
gray-green leaves.
🄰◊
F. imperialis p.17
F. imperialis
'The Premier' *p.45*
F. imperialis 'Rubra' *p. 45*
F. pallidiflora p.18

G

Galanthus (Snowdrop)
This genus of small bulbs has
white, bell-shaped flowers.
Most are spring flowering,
but a few flower in autumn.
G. elwesii is a small plant,
but it is a robust grower, with
broad, glaucous leaves and a
white, nodding flower. It likes
a little more sun than some

GALANTHUS PLICATUS
subsp. *BYZANTINUS*

snowdrops. When happy, it regularly sets seed.

G. nivalis (Common snowdrop) is a beautiful harbinger of spring and can become naturalized. It has a nodding, white flower with a small green ring on the inside. The leaves are quite narrow. These snowdrops are easy to cultivate and to naturalize.

G. plicatus is a large snowdrop with turned-back margins to the leaves. This bulb quickly develops offsets. ▣◊Z3-9

Also recommended: G. 'S. Arnott'

Galtonia

A small South African genus of summer-growing bulbs that are well suited to a herbaceous border or containers. *G. candicans* is a medium plant that flowers in late summer. The head of up to 30 white, pendulous flowers is surrounded by long, gray-green leaves. Not dormant until well into autumn, it may be sold in pots just before flowering. ▣◊Z7-10

IRISES

This is a large genus of bulbous and rhizomatous plants available in many shapes and colors. The Reticulata irises have simple netted bulbs, whereas the Juno irises have bulbs with long, fleshy roots. Xiphium irises flower later in spring and have larger bulbs.

Juno iris
I. bucharica is a vigorous iris of medium stature with glossy, broad leaves, beneath which are produced several large, creamy white flowers with yellow blades on the falls (the large, spreading outer petals). A sunny position with good, free-draining soil is best. ▣◊Z5-9

Reticulata irises
'Harmony', a small iris, is ideal for growing in containers or on the edge of a border. The flowers are royal blue with a yellow area on the falls.

IRIS 'HARMONY'

IRIS BUCHARICA

'J.S. Dijt' is a small iris that never fails to flower in late winter if planted in a sunny position. It has rich purple flowers with orange marks on the falls.

'Katharine Hodgkin' This unusually colored, small, bulbous iris was discovered in an English garden. It has distinctive, light blue flowers with a mix of yellow and blue on the falls. A strong grower, this iris is invaluable for brightening up a gloomy late winter day, and it is capable of withstanding the vagaries of winter. ▣◊Z5-8

Also recommended: 'Joyce'

Xiphium iris
I. latifolia, a medium iris from northern Spain, has violet flowers with yellow markings on the falls. ▣◊Z7-9

GLADIOLUS 'MI MI'

Gladiolus
A widespread genus of cormous perennials from Africa and southern Europe. Where not hardy, they are planted in spring and lifted when the leaves begin to turn yellow. There are many selections of these tall plants with showy, open funnel-shaped flowers in midsummer. They can be planted in borders or used in a more formal setting. 'Mi Mi' has deep pink flowers with white centers. ▣◊Z 8 - 10
G. communis subsp. **byzantinus** *p.37*
Also recommended: *G. tristis*

H

Hippeastrum (Amaryllis)
These medium bulbs are from South America and can be stored at precise temperatures to flower at almost any time of the year, particularly in winter and spring. They have smallish to large, trumpet-shaped flowers, in varying shades from white to deep red and in combinations, on thick stems. In colder climates, they are ideal container plants, suitable for a sunny window-sill or conservatory. ▣◊☙

Hyacinthoides (Bluebell)
These vigorous bulbs pull themselves deeply into the soil with contractile roots. They grow well in most situations. *H. hispanica* (syn. *Scilla hispanica*, Spanish bluebell) is of medium height and very tolerant of many garden positions. It is excellent in a wilder setting, such as a woodland or an orchard. The mid-blue flowers grow in a spire, with each one curving back at the tips.
H. non-scripta (syn. *Scilla non-scripta*, English bluebell) is a vigorous, medium-height bulb, similar to *H. hispanica* but with backward curving, blue flowers held on one side of the flower spike only. The glossy leaves are dark green and arch out from the base to frame the plant. If you do not want a large colony, remove the flowerheads before the seed is set. This bulb is also available in both white and pink forms. ▣◊Z 4 - 9

HIPPEASTRUM 'APPLE BLOSSOM'

HYACINTHOIDES NON-SCRIPTA

Hyacinthus (Hyacinth)
A familiar bulb. All of the cultivars derive from the smaller and refined species *H. orientalis*. Dutch growers have been selecting these larger-flowered forms for over a hundred years, particularly for the forced flower market. *H. orientalis*, the ubiquitous hyacinth, is small in stature and available in a wide range of colors from white through pink to red, purple, and violet. Shades of yellow and apricot are also found. These are first-class bulbs for formal bedding in spring or for containers, which can be prepared for early flowering. *H. orientalis* 'Anna Marie' has fragrant, tubular, bell-shaped pink flowers held in a tight spike. This selection is particularly good for forcing. *H. orientalis* 'Delft Blue' is a single, soft blue form. *H. orientalis* 'White Pearl' is a slightly later, pure white, single-flowered selection. ▣◊Z 5 - 9
'Carnegie' *p.45*
'City of Haarlem' *p.45*
'L'Innocence' *p.45*
'Ostara' *p.45*

LILIUM (LILIES)

Lily hybrids are easier to cultivate than the species. However, the flowers of the species do have an allure and grace that is seldom found in the hybrids. Plant them in a deep hole incorporating organic matter. Lilies need staking only in windy sites, and most are ideal for pots with adequate root space.

Asiatic hybrids

'Connecticut King' is a tall, unscented lily with long-lasting, upward-facing, yellow flowers in summer.
'Enchantment' is prolific in the garden and good for cutting. In summer, this medium lily has unscented, upward-facing, orange flowers that curve back.
'Mont Blanc' is a medium, summer-flowering, vigorous lily and has white, upward-facing, unscented flowers with brown spots.
'Red Night' (syn. 'Roter Cardinal') is a medium lily with upward-

LILIUM 'JOURNEY'S END'

facing, unscented flowers in early summer. It has light, black spots in the center. ⬛◊Z 3 - 8

Oriental hybrids

'Casa Blanca' has pure white, bowl-shaped flowers produced in summer in clusters on tall stems. They are scented and have contrasting dark orange anthers.
'Journey's End' is an unusual combination of pink and maroon, with white margins. This tall, broad and backward curving lily has very attractive, unscented flowers in late summer. ⬛◊Z 4 - 8

Trumpet hybrids

Golden Splendor Group lilies are tall trumpet lilies with dark, scented, yellow flowers veined with deep red. A summer-flowering, vigorous plant that rarely needs staking. ⬛◊Z 5 - 7

Species

L. *martagon* (Common turkscap lily) is tall with shiny, unpleasant smelling, pink to purple turkscap flowers in early and midsummer. The dark green leaves grow in whorls. In the white form the leaves are apple green. ▣ – ⬛◊Z 3 - 7
L. *regale* (Regal lily) is a tall Chinese lily. It has white, scented trumpet-shaped flowers stained brown-purple on the outside in midsummer. It needs full sun and rich soil for best results. ⬛◊Z 4 - 7
L. *speciosum* var. *rubrum* needs acidic, moist soil. Its tall, dark stems have scented, pendulous, turkscap flowers of rich carmine marked with dark spots in late summer and early autumn. ⬛◊Z 4 - 8
L. *superbum* (American turkscap lily) is tall with unscented, orange-red, spotted flowers in autumn. The leaves grow in whorls. ⬛◊Z 4 - 7

LILIUM 'RED NIGHT'

LILIUM REGALE

I

Ipheion

A small genus of bulbs from the eastern side of South America. They are related to onions and give off a familiar smell when the leaves are crushed, but the flowers, produced in spring, are often honey-scented.

I. uniflorum 'Wisley Blue' is an attractive little bulb well worth trying in gardens. Ipheion is small with light blue, star-shaped flowers and dense, grasslike leaves. It multiplies quickly and is useful when planted between shrubs or at the edge of a rock garden. ▨◊Z6-9

L

Leucojum (Snowflake)

The snowflakes are rather neglected. The three kinds described here are easy to grow and quick to multiply.

L. aestivum 'Gravetye Giant' (Summer snowflake) is a medium-growing bulbous plant with glossy green, strap-shaped leaves and stems with up to eight white, pendulous green-tipped bells. This bulb is excellent in full sun by a pond or in partial shade in a border. It may need a little support if planted in an exposed position. ▨◊Z4-9

L. autumnale is a delicate-looking, but hardy, small plant suitable for a raised bed or rock garden. The ½in (1cm) bell-shaped flowers are among the first flowers of autumn. They start to appear in late summer and are soon

LEUCOJUM AESTIVUM 'GRAVETYE GIANT'

followed by the grasslike leaves. ▨◊Z5-9

L. vernum (Spring snowflake) A small but robust plant with quite short strap-shaped leaves that are produced with the flowers in early spring. These flowers are open and bell-shaped and are white with green or yellow tips. Spring snowflakes provide a taller-growing alternative to snowdrops. ▨◊Z4-8

M

Muscari (Grape hyacinth)

Grape hyacinths are a group of easily cultivated bulbs, generally producing blue or white flowers in spring. They are well suited to almost all gardens and will soon spread to colonize an area. Grape hyacinths may be forced for winter bloom indoors.

M. armeniacum is a vigorous, small plant with spikes of bright-blue, bell-like flowers with constricted white mouths appearing in spring. The thin, strap-

MUSCARI ARMENIACUM

shaped leaves are produced in autumn. This bulb is ideal for planting in wild or isolated parts of the garden, where its spreading habit may be an asset. ▨◊Z4-8

M. azureum, syn. *Hyacinthus azureus*, is a small bulb with upright, grayish leaves and is well suited to rock gardens, where the bright blue flowers can be appreciated. It may seed prolifically, so it is good for producing drifts of color in spring borders. ▨◊Z7-10

M. latifolium is a small, spring-flowering plant with just one or two broad leaves and a strikingly bicolored spike of violet-black, fertile florets at the base and pale blue infertile florets above. Slower growing than most grape hyacinths and not as vigorous as some varieties. ▨◊Z4-8

M. macrocarpum is also small in stature but has large, yellow, highly fragrant flowers in spring. This bulb needs a hot, dry, well-drained position to grow well and is ideally suited to a raised bed. ▨◊Z7-9

NARCISSUS (DAFFODILS)

The range of daffodils on offer is vast. The shape and color of each cultivar is clear from the illustrations in catalogs and garden centres. Equally important, however, is the height – some large-flowered daffodils need plenty of space and require careful placing. The varieties listed here are mostly medium in stature and easily cultivated. Buy daffodils as soon as they go on sale, because the roots will begin to grow in late summer. Most are hardy throughout most of North America.

Daffodils for borders
'Cheerfulness' has a sweetly scented, double white flower with creamy yellow petals forming the trumpet. It is a medium height bulb and has mid-season flowers.
'Dove Wings' has white, swept-back outer petals and a lemon yellow trumpet. This is a very small but

NARCISSUS 'CHEERFULNESS'

sturdy, free-flowering bulb. 'February Gold' often begins flowering in very early spring. It has a stunning all gold-colored, medium flower, with a darker trumpet.
'Irene Copeland' has a double flower with white outer petals and a bright yellow double trumpet. It grows to medium height and flowers in mid-spring.
'Jack Snipe' is a small plant with white outer petals and a lemon yellow trumpet. It flowers well and bulks up very quickly.
'Jetfire' is also small and has a good contrast between its yellow outer petals and bright orange trumpet. At first the trumpet is quite pale in color but soon darkens with time.
'Minnow' is a small, multi-headed, scented narcissus with pale yellow trumpets surrounded by cream outer petals. This daffodil is best grown in a large container or a raised bed.
'Mount Hood' is a medium-height daffodil with a cream trumpet and whiter outer petals. It has a mid-spring flower of good substance.
'Pipit' is a scented, medium-height daffodil, with two to three lemon flowers per stem.
'Tête-à-Tête' is small but vigorous, with up to three flowers per stem. It has yellow outer petals and a golden trumpet.
'Thalia' has a neat, creamy white flower with a small, open trumpet of medium height. A prolific plant, it

NARCISSUS 'TÊTE-À-TÊTE'

will flower regularly without being lifted.
⊞◊

Daffodils for forcing
N. papyraceus has a white form available in autumn, sold as 'Paper White', to flower in midwinter. Of medium height, it produces small but fragrant, white flowers. It does well in mild gardens. ⊞◊ Z 8 - 9 (Also try 'Jack Snipe', 'Minnow' and 'Tête-à-Tête')

Daffodils for naturalizing
N. poeticus var. recurvus (Old pheasant's eye) This medium-height daffodil has white outer petals and small, red-rimmed, yellow cups.
N. pseudonarcissus (syn. N. lobularis, Lent lily, Wild daffodil) This is a small but willing naturalizer from Europe. It is a classic daffodil, with nodding yellow trumpets and cream outer petals.
⊞◊ (Also try 'February Gold' or many others.)

NERINE BOWDENII

N

Nerine

A South African genus of small to medium bulbs that flower in autumn in the Northern hemisphere, nerines are dormant during the dry summer, flowering in autumn with the leaves emerging afterward. There are many hybrids that are excellent for conservatories or containers. Where winters are mild, some thrive in sheltered niches.
N. bowdenii is under-rated for the autumn, being small in stature but with large clusters of lilylike, pink flowers on sturdy stems. The bulbs should be planted shallowly on the sunny side of a wall, where they will flower year after year with very little attention. They are excellent cut flowers. ⊠◊Z8-10

O

Ornithogalum (Star-of-Bethlehem)

A large genus with a few spring-flowering, sturdy representatives that are easy to grow in most situations.
O. nutans A mid-spring flowering, small bulb with silvery white, pendent, bell-shaped flowers held in a one-sided spike. These are held above slightly succulent leaves with a central silver stripe. A quietly attractive plant to place close to the path or border's edge, to be viewed at close quarters.
O. umbellatum (Star-of-Bethlehem) A tough, small plant, ideal for areas where little else will grow, such as the base of hedges or tight against a building. In good growing conditions, it may increase too rapidly. The starry, white flowers have a green stripe externally and form a dense cluster. ⊠-▨◊Z6-10
O. pyrenaicum p.37
Also recommended:
O. narbonense

Oxalis (Shamrock, Sorrel)

A huge genus of very varied plants, all with very similar five-petaled flowers that are twisted in the bud stage.
O. adenophylla is a very small

OXALIS ADENOPHYLLA

bulb from South America that will grow well in a rock garden or large container. It has a wide, funnel-shaped, single, dark pink flower with a paler center, produced in late spring. ⊠◊Z6-8

P

Puschkinia

A small, spring-flowering genus from western Asia, needing a well-drained site.
P. scilloides is a small bulb with two upright leaves and tight heads of pale blue, open, bell-shaped flowers with a darker blue line down the center of each petal. This is a very adaptable plant that will grow in full sun or partial shade. ⊠-▨◊Z3-9

S

Scilla

This are good bulbs for bringing a true blue to the garden in early spring.
S. bifolia is a small bulb that

SCILLA BIFOLIA

will brighten up any part of the garden in early spring with its bluish, starry flowers. The dark green leaves are sparse and have a hooked tip. There are also white and pink forms. ⊞◊Z 3 - 8

S. peruviana Despite the name, this bulb hails from the western Mediterranean. It is small and unusual in that it is virtually evergreen – its many tapering leaves are produced in the autumn, long before it blooms in early summer in a many-flowered, conical, violet-blue or white flowerhead. ⊞◊Z 8 - 9

S. siberica 'Spring Beauty', syn. 'Atrocoerulea', is a little taller than *S. bifolia* and has deep blue, more pendent flowers in early spring. It looks very effective when planted around deciduous shrubs or in conjunction with white or red flowers. ⊞◊Z 5 - 8

Sternbergia
(Autumn daffodil)
This bulb provides a welcome and stunning contrast to the predominantly pink flowers of other autumnal bulbs.

S. lutea is a small plant for a sunny spot. In autumn, it has bright yellow, goblet-shaped flowers, surrounded by dark green, narrow, strap-shaped leaves. This is a tough little plant, and it will continue to flower well into winter if the weather is mild. ⊞◊Z 7 - 9

S. sicula is a small bulb that has bright, butter yellow flowers. It demands a hot, sunny spot, where the thin, dark green leaves contrast well with the yellow goblet-shaped flowers. ⊞◊Z 6 - 9

TULIPA (TULIPS)

This popular genus of perennial, spring-flowering bulbs revels in sunny, warm conditions during the summer. It may be necessary to lift the bulbs in late spring and replant them in the autumn, depending on the conditions in your garden. There are hundreds of cultivars to choose from. ⊞◊Z 4 - 7

Bowl-shaped flowers
T. linifolia Batalinii Group
These are small to medium, early-flowering tulips that come in red, yellow, apricot, and bronze. They are very easy to grow in a well-drained spot.

T. praestans 'Fusilier' is a barely medium-height tulip that is particularly easily grown and very reliable. It has several vibrant, red flowers on each stem.

Tulipa batalinii

'Red Riding Hood' is a small tulip that has attractive green leaves marked with dark maroon patches. The outside of the flower is red, but inside it is scarlet with a black base.

Single cup-shaped flowers
'Attila' is of medium height with a single, pink-violet flower. It grows well in pots and can be planted closely or with annuals.

'Queen of Night' is a medium tulip that flowers later in the season, with very dark maroon flowers and plain green leaves. It is effective alongside white flowers.

Goblet-shaped flowers
'Queen of Sheba' is a medium-height, late-flowering tulip, with red flowers edged with orange.

Also recommended:
T. sprengeri

Tulipa 'Queen of Sheba'

INDEX

ACKNOWLEDGMENTS

Picture research Anna Grapes
  Mariana Sonnenberg
Picture librarians Richard Dabb
  Romaine Werblow

Planting plan llustrations Anne Winterbotham
Additional illustration Sharon Moore

Index Chris Bernstein

Dorling Kindersley would like to thank:
All staff at the RHS, in particular Susanne Mitchell, Karen Wilson and Barbara Haynes at Vincent Square. Thanks also to Joanna Chisholm for editorial assistance.

Studio Cactus would like to thank:
Susi Bailey, Alison Bolus, Sue Gordon, and Kate Hayward for editorial assistance; Lesley Malkin for proofreading; Alison Donovan, Claire Pegrum, Ann Thompson, and Laura Watson for design assistance. Thanks also to Mr. and Mrs. Lunn and Mr. and Mrs. Trown for the use of their gardens.

The American Horticultural Society
Visit AHS at www.ahs.org or call them at 1-800-777-7931 ext. 199. Membership benefits include *The American Gardener* magazine, free admission to flower shows, the free seed exchange, book services, and the Gardener's Information Service.

Photography
The publisher would also like to thank the following for their kind permission to reproduce their photographs:
(key: t=top, c=center, b=below, l=left, r=right)
Sue Atkinson: 3
Jonathan Buckley: 23tl.
Jacqui Hurst: 64
Rod Leeds: 9tl, 11cr, 33bl.
Harry Smith Collection: 15bl.